Gabby

Gabby

The little dog that had to learn to bark

BARBY KEEL

CITADEL PRESS
Kensington Publishing Corp.
www.kensingtonbooks.com

CITADEL PRESS BOOKS are published by

Kensington Publishing Corp.
119 West 40th Street
New York, NY 10018

All Kensington titles, imprints, and distributed lines are available at special quantity discounts for bulk purchases for sales promotions, premiums, fund-raising, educational, or institutional use.

Special book excerpts or customized printings can also be created to fit specific needs. For details, write or phone the office of the Kensington sales manager: Kensington Publishing Corp., 119 West 40th Street, New York, NY 10018, attn: Sales Department; phone 1-800-221-2647.

CITADEL PRESS and the Citadel logo are Reg. U.S. Pat. & TM Off.

ISBN-13: 978-0-8065-4032-0
ISBN-10: 0-8065-4032-X

First Citadel trade paperback printing: February 2020

10 9 8 7 6 5 4 3 2

Printed in the United States of America

Electronic edition:

ISBN-13: 978-0-8065-4033-7(e-book)
ISBN-10: 0-8065-4033-8 (e-book)

For Christine,
who died on March 10, 2012,
after suffering from cancer

CONTENTS

INTRODUCTION

The first dog I was ever able to call my own was a handsome mongrel called Rex. At least, *I* thought he was gorgeous-looking. In reality he was a rather mangy mixture of breeds, with a lopsided grin and cream-colored fur, patches of it missing in places.

It was 1945, and I was ten years old. It wasn't long after VE Day, which marked the end of the Second World War in Europe, and everyone, including us children, was still giddy with the sense of victory and freedom. One day I arrived home from school to find a dog in the kitchen lapping at a bowl of water. It was love at first sight.

From the moment I set eyes on Rex, he was my dog, even though it was my father who had found this stray hound and had taken him in off the streets. Dad was soppy when it came to animals—and I inherited his love for them. Many times during my formative years he would come home from his work as a chef at a small hotel carrying an animal he'd "rescued" from one of the shabby pet shops that used to exist in those days. He came home with cats, dogs, and even a monkey and a bush baby! I grew up watching him devote his tenderness to any stray or sick creature within our neighborhood in Eastbourne, Sussex, and I vowed to do the same when I was "grown up."

To this day, I remember seeing Rex peering out of the front room window, waiting for my return from school. As I opened the front door, I could hear the scratch of his paws scrabbling to gain purchase on the wooden floors, and he would bound up to me, covering me in doggie kisses and rendering me helpless with giggles. We were inseparable. Every night he slept on my bed, and every day he pined as I left for school, just as I pined being away from him as the school day dragged on. I longed for the bell that heralded the end of lessons, and I would skip all the way home to be reunited with him.

I didn't have the easiest of childhoods, and perhaps that's why animals became my focus, as a way of dealing with that. But mostly I think I was born with a passion for them that has surpassed everything else. As a child, my relationship with my mother was fraught, to say the least. I was never her favorite child. She made it very clear that she preferred my older brother Peter to me, and then our (much) younger sister Pam, who appeared ten years after I was born. It was Mum who made the decision to put Rex to sleep one day when I was at school. Rex was old, and he hadn't been himself for the weeks leading up to that day. Even so, it was a huge shock to come home from class and find the house empty, my beloved dog taken from me without a word to me. Never again would I hear him rushing to greet me. Never again would I feel his cold wet nose against my face as he showed me the kind of devotion only a dog can. Never again would I curl up in bed with him, feeling his heart beating and the warmth of his rangy body against mine as we drifted off to sleep. It was an unforgiveable act, in my eyes, and I don't think I ever truly forgave her. That night, and for many nights after, I cried myself to sleep. My heart was completely broken at the loss of my first-ever pet, and I can still recall his dear face today, so many years later.

Luckily, I had Dad. He was the kindest, gentlest man in the world, and he was my refuge during my mother's storms, which broke over my head all too frequently. It wasn't just my immediate family life that was difficult. I was four when war broke out and can remember bombing raids by the Luft-waffe, and I was once almost gunned down in a field while being evacuated. My love of animals got me through. I even had a pet in our air-raid shelter, a frog I nicknamed Prince Charming, and those nights when we were all huddled inside, wondering if we would survive, I would croon over that small, green frog.

Animals, unlike humans, generally have simple needs; to be loved, to be cared for, to be fed and watered and given a soft bed to sleep on. During my life, animals, and especially my pet dogs, have soothed the parts of me left wounded by my childhood, have healed me in ways that are profound.

At the Animal Sanctuary that I run in Bexhill, Sussex, we recognize that it isn't just the animals that are saved by our care. I believe passionately in the power of animals to heal *us*. The connection between beasts and mankind is as old as time itself. When an animal comes to the sanctuary and is nurtured back to health, we are all changed in meaningful ways. We are all made a little better by the experience.

The animals who come to us are often victims of neglect or downright cruelty. They are abandoned, unwanted, possibly ill and in pain. We make no judgment about the humans responsible, as far as we are able, as the animal is always at the center of our thinking. Love is the core of everything we do day by day, hour by hour. It is love that drives us forward, it is the reason we keep going. Every day there are new animals who come in needing our love and care, and every day we make sure we give it to them. It is rare that an animal doesn't respond, but always in their own way and in their own time.

I never intended to set up an animal sanctuary. In fact, I almost became a model in London when I was a young woman in my twenties. It was 1958 and the age of glamour had arrived after the years of post-war austerity. Suddenly Hollywood film stars were aspired to, and the newspapers and magazines were full of beautiful actresses and handsome actors. At the time, I had a slim figure with blonde hair styled in a fashionable updo on my head. I was offered the chance to model for Coca-Cola. A photographer, who was scouting the Sussex coast for models, spotted me in the line of a fish and chip shop. He stopped me as I left, two big bundles of chips wrapped in newspaper in my arms, and offered me the chance to go to London, all expenses paid.

I realize now that it was probably the pivotal moment in my life, though I didn't know it then. I stood there, gawping at the man holding out his business card, and without a second's thought I turned it down. He was holding out the prospect of fame and fortune, of glamour and possibly wealth, but I knew even at that formative age that it just wasn't me. I didn't want to leave my dad and go off with a stranger to a big city. I liked it where I was and I couldn't have cared less about following fashion or big brands, though I liked to make myself look nice as any young woman did back then. I was—and still am—a country girl, happier in a muddy field shifting a bale of straw than posing for pictures.

It was the right decision. It took another thirteen years, but eventually I saw some land on Freezeland Lane, Bexhill, Sussex, put up for sale. It cost £1,500 for four acres, and this time I knew it was what I wanted. I had been saving up for years with the intention of buying a plot, and this was my opportunity. I was with my former partner Les at the time. I drove him out there, parked, and stepped outside. It was a warm spring day, the kind that holds the magic of possibility. The trees were bursting with life. The grass was lush like the rolling countryside that surrounded us. I breathed in the smell of the soil beneath our feet, and I knew I had to buy the land. I felt instantly at home. Even though we were only a couple of miles from Bexhill town center, it felt like we were deep in the country with fields and farmland for miles around.

My father had separated from my mother by then, so, in 1971, I gathered up my few possessions, my bush baby and two dogs, and started a new life, with Dad in tow. United in our love for the outdoors and caring for our four-legged friends, we decided to take in a few strays, just a few, to look after on the land. I put two trailers on the site, one for me and Les, the other for my father. I'll always remember the smile on Les's handsome face that day, reflecting back my happiness. I was thirty-six at the time, and I had no career plan. I don't think such a thing existed back then. They were simpler times; you grew up, got a job, and settled down with someone. I hadn't quite done things in that order, but it was the right time for me to put down roots at last.

I named the land "Pipzedene" after the three animals that started it all: Pip was a golden spaniel with an infectious, exuberant personality; Zede was a black-and-tan German shepherd, extremely loyal but quite reserved, while Deana was my gray bush baby. I built up the site brick by brick, fence by fence, over the years. Very soon after moving in, I started taking in animals. As time went on, I had to create enclosures, then pens, then pathways and more fencing, as the variety of animals under my wing increased. From those small humble beginnings, the Animal Sanctuary was born.

It grew organically. I knew that for many people, my shelter was a last resort, the final place they could come before an animal was put down or heartlessly dumped. My soft heart and inability to say no to a suffering creature have meant that over the years, I have fostered hundreds, perhaps thousands, of animals of all descriptions. We've had donkeys, horses, ponies, goats, sheep, cows, pigs, chickens, ducks, geese, guinea fowl, pigeons, peacocks, seagulls, gerbils, guinea pigs, mice, chinchilla, rabbits, and ferrets come to us, alongside the cats and dogs for rehoming. We usually have two hundred cats at any one time.

Over time, people started contacting me asking to volunteer, and so my staff grew. Then, as the bills began pouring in, and the makeshift sanctuary looked on the verge of collapse, we were saved many times by supporters bequeathing money to the shelter in their wills. Donations started trickling in, and so we set up an animal sponsorship scheme and asked for donations from those rehoming cats or dogs, largely toward the cost of spaying or neutering the animals. Against all the odds, we kept growing, and we soon had roughly four hundred animals in our care. In the same year we became a registered charity.

On some days, we'd have as many as six cats, two dogs, and several sheep given to us; on others we'd have a crateful of hens that had escaped the chop at the end of their laying lives, an injured pheasant, a pig that had been seen by a member of the public abandoned in a farmer's field. It was an endless roll of variety—with many sad stories woven into the menagerie. Every day I see animals that have been neglected, and often worse—dumped over our gate, beaten, starved, or sometimes even dying. I am a tough bird, but the horrors I've witnessed, inflicted on blameless animals, have broken my heart time and time again over the years. Yet I also see the best of human kindness with my motley crew, as I call my staff of volunteers, giving these poor creatures the love, care, and shelter they need. Many require medical treatment when they arrive here. Many just need to live out their last days in peace and comfort, though we try to rehome as many animals as possible but only to loving and permanent families. Any animal that cannot be found a place to live is given a place here at the sanctuary. No creature is turned away.

Fostering animals is a privilege, and I couldn't imagine doing anything else with my life. My house is permanently filled with volunteers, dogs, and visitors, and I wouldn't have it any other way. To protect the identities of those involved, I have changed some names and identifying features of both animals and humans, but the facts of each case are true, and offer a revealing insight into the world of caring for unwanted animals.

I wanted to write this book to give people an honest account of my life as an animal fosterer, to show the struggles and challenges I face on a daily basis, and to show that with love and care, many animals can be saved and healed at my sanctuary, and at many other good sanctuaries around the country, and how, in turn, we, too, are healed in ways that are beyond words.

Chapter 1

NEW ARRIVALS

The day dawned with bright summer light that glowed across the fields, the enclosures, and the landscape that surrounded us. Though we were only a short distance from the town center, it felt like we were a million miles away on mornings like this. Apart from the electricity transmission lines that sliced through the land, it was a rural idyll, and it felt like we were somehow apart from civilization. The backdrop to my life was the rolling, undulating Sussex countryside, and, of course, the sanctuary land that sheltered and housed animals of every description. I breathed in the smell of summer, that indefinable scent of flowers and grass, which mixed with the familiar sanctuary aroma of fresh straw, dry fur, and mud.

I yawned. The residents of the sanctuary had started their waking rituals at 4 A.M.: the roosters crowed as they struck their funny poses around the yard, the pigs grunted, the horses brayed in the back fields, the goats and sheep bleated for their breakfast. Then there were the dogs barking in the kennels, desperate for a walk, and the noise from the assorted ducks, geese, chickens, and seagulls that also resided here. Their squawks, clucks, honks, and screeches joined the cacophony, making me smile. It was just another day at the Animal Sanctuary.

"I'd better get up and make Dan some beans on toast. He'll be in for his breakfast soon," I muttered to myself as I hastily got dressed. My mind was already whirring from the list of jobs I had to get on with that morning. "I need to check with Diane about the cat who may be deaf. He's due to be rehomed soon, and so we must get him to the vet to check. The pigs need new straw, so I'll do that first. Those bundles are blimmin' heavy for an old lady like myself!" I chuckled.

I laughed because even though I was sixty-eight years old, I was fighting fit. Every morning at daybreak I'd get up, pull on a top and some trousers, and head out to clean out the animals, dragging huge sacks of goat or sheep feed, pulling a bale of hay onto my back or striding over the fields in search of a missing goat. I never felt my age. I'd spent my life working hard, and it didn't occur to me for a minute that I might retire one day. Why would I want to sit around with nothing to do? That would kill me faster than any hard labor, or so I thought.

I'd bought this land thirty-one years ago with a view to taking in a few unwanted or abandoned animals or strays. Within a few months of setting up in my leaky RV on the site, the trickle of strays had turned into a deluge, with the horses, goats, dogs, and donkeys all roaming free, as animals should be, on my land. All I had to contain them was a fence that ran around the perimeter of the site, which I'd sold my car as well as canceled my life insurance to help pay for. I figured that without children, I had no one to inherit anything anyway. That's how daft I've always been about animals—I'd do anything to help them.

"Are you doing my breakfast, Barby? Not a problem if not," smiled Dan, as he ambled in.

Dan always had a twinkle in his eye, always teasing me in his gentle way. He was our farm manager and took care of the larger beasts. He was one of my most trusted staff, a tall man in his early thirties with dark hair and glasses, quietly spoken and utterly capable, though I berated him often for his "laid-back" attitude. I am pretty feisty, as any of my volunteers would testify, but underneath it I'm also a worrier— and his calm approach to the dramas we encountered here on a daily basis drove me crazy at times. We would have badly treated animals being dumped here, six or seven unwanted cats arriving every day, animals always needing medical attention, sometimes urgently, and this all combined to make me feel overwhelmed at times. Dan, who had worked here for six years, would shrug his shoulders and get on with the task in hand, in his own way and in his own time. Probably because of our differences, we made a good team.

"There you go, here's your breakfast," I said, handing Dan a plate of steaming hot baked beans. "There's toast in the toaster. Now I'd better get on and look at those documents from yesterday before I go out . . ." I always made him his breakfast. It was part of our routine. He did all the big, dirty jobs on the site, so it was my small way of showing appreciation.

Wandering into the living room of my sprawling bungalow,

I spotted a pile of forms that I needed to attend to. Every time an animal such as a cat or dog is brought to the rescue center, the previous owners have to sign a form signing away any rights they have over their pet to the Animal Sanctuary. We have strict procedures in place to make sure that each animal is properly registered, given immediate medical attention if needed, and either spayed or neutered to prevent any more unwanted creatures coming into the world. Animals such as pigs, deer, sheep, cows, and goats are subject to a Defra Movement General Licence, which means that we have to follow government guidelines, whereas our forms for cats and dogs are more of a formality than an official requirement, but it gives us the confidence and assurance that the animals were being handed to us completely, and that after the seven-day cooling-off period, they become our legal responsibility.

It has to be this way. The number of people who ring up after a few months because they've changed their minds and want their pet back is astonishing. We feel the animals are best served by stability, care, and rehoming as quickly as possible into loving, permanent homes. It can be an emotional, and often extremely difficult, decision to give up a beloved pet, and we understand how traumatic it can be, for humans and animals alike, which is why we have processes in place to mitigate that stress for everyone. Animals need love, care, the right food, and exercise, and we know that circumstances change and this can become a burden. Pets develop behavioral problems, or fall ill and need expensive medical treatment, which forces families in poverty to say good-bye, but we also know that some people simply don't want their animal, or have grown tired of the expense and commitment.

We're always here to pick up the pieces and take in these unwanted pets, otherwise what would happen to them? God only knows. Yet, I always dread having to go through the paperwork!

Just as I sat down, a steaming cup of tea in my hand, shuffling that pile of documents, something caught my eye—a swift, sharp movement outside. I peered out through the sliding glass door that led out into a small sunroom beyond the living room. I blinked and was greeted by a blaze of color. Emerald green feathers resplendent in the sunshine, a tall azure neck, and a crest of shimmering feathers over the peacock's head. I stood for a moment, spellbound.

"Dan, Dan, are you there, dear?" He'd wolfed down his meal and had already left by the time I came out of the reverie this magnificent creature had sent me into. I clutched my walkie-talkie to my mouth. It was the simplest way of reaching my staff and volunteers across the four-acre site.

A man's voice spoke, crackling: "Barby, all okay?"

"Dan, would you please come back over to the house? I've got a surprise for you . . ." I almost laughed with delight.

The peacock was proudly strutting around my yard, forcing the chickens and geese that roamed free to scatter, clucking with indignation as they went. The magnificent bird, a glorious creature, was already looking very "at home" in the sanctuary.

Dan appeared from the direction of the farm animal enclosures that lay beyond my gaze. He stopped for a moment just to look. I watched him gaze at the peacock before he turned to come into the house. My place was a single-story bungalow with one "upstairs" room, which was used for storage, more of an attic than a proper room. Over the years, I'd added an annex that had housed my father until he died at the grand old age of ninety-six, and a sunroom for both myself and Dad. I had a covered area to the right of my front door, which was on the southern side, with shaded seating for our visitors during the summer months. Once inside, the front door opened into a short corridor that led to the kitchen, with my lounge on the left and my bedroom farther up the hallway. It wasn't a big place but it was just right for me. My living room was always rather full, with filing cabinets, a sofa and armchairs for volunteers to drink their break-time cuppas, and a huge glass-fronted cabinet filled to the brim with my darts trophies. Animals weren't my only passion. I'd played for darts teams for decades and had won many a shiny cup or shield, and they were a source of huge pride to me.

"Well, we've definitely got a new peacock!" Dan said as he marched into the living room.

"Do you reckon he's one of those that went astray?" I asked, referring to the fact that a wealthy couple had decided to give up their muster of peacocks two years previously after finding that, although they looked beautiful, they made a hell of a lot of noise.

"Well, we had three or four peacocks left with us by that couple, so perhaps so. This one may have run off and somehow survived scavenging until now," said Dan, rubbing his chin thoughtfully.

We both looked back at the incredible bird that had now dropped his crowning glory of feathers and was stalking off toward the cattery.

"He's a beauty, that's for sure," I murmured, "and I'm going to call him Peter. Peter the Peacock."

"Alright, Barby," Dan interjected. "I'm off to feed the pigs. They've been given the new straw, so you don't have to worry about that. They're already busy making it into their bed."

Pigs are amazing creatures. All you do is dump the straw in the middle of their pen, and they will create their own sleeping area, which they never foul, making them one of the cleanest animals there is.

"Okay Dan, thank you, dear," I replied, still lost in thought.

There was something magical about peacocks—and strangely, I felt a pull toward this one. Perhaps that's why I'd chosen to name him after my beloved brother, who died at the tragically early age of fifty-eight, twelve years ago, though it still felt like yesterday. He'd had leukemia. He had been too young to die, and here I still was, aged sixty-eight and still going strong. I missed him every single day. He was my older brother by two years, and the person I had been closest to in the world, apart from Dad. Life just wasn't fair sometimes. My brother hadn't been a particular fan of peacocks, so I had no idea why I named the creature after him—except the desire to remember and appreciate something so otherworldly. I've always been sentimental—about animals mostly—but when it came to my brother, there was no limit to my love, and it spilled out in ways like this.

My musing was broken by the phone ringing. I probably fielded twenty to thirty calls a day.

"Hello, can I help you?"

"Hello, I'm ringing on behalf of my relatives. They're very elderly and are having to go into a home. They have four dogs. The greyhound and gorgeous Lhasa Apso are being rehomed, but we still have two that we can't find places for. Could you please take them?"

I paused for a second. My mind flitted straight from Peter and the peacock to this new dilemma. That's how life worked here. We never had a second to think. I wasn't sure we had room in the kennels, but instantly I couldn't bear the thought of those poor dogs being left without anywhere to go.

"I'll speak to Fran, who helps look after the dogs, but I'm pretty sure we'll have them. What breeds are they?"

"Kenny is a Jack Russell, and Jessy is a Yorkshire terrier. We'd be so grateful if you could help us."

"We'll make room for them somehow, don't worry," I replied. "When can you bring them in?"

The arrangements were made, and as soon as the phone call had ended, I buzzed through to Fran, who was out feeding the horses. Fran was a stocky, fair-haired man who came in a couple of days a week and had only been working at the sanctuary for a few months. He confirmed that the kennels were full. At that point I had a brainstorm and dived for my book. This book was the heart of the sanctuary, as it contained all the phone numbers and names of anyone who had ever rung to ask about taking in cats or dogs. I leafed through it.

"Bingo!" I said out loud.

Reaching for the phone, I dialed the number.

"Hello, dear. Do you still want two terriers?" I didn't need to stand on ceremony, as the woman who wanted to rehome two dogs was an old pal of mine, Ivy.

The lady's response was an unequivocal yes!

"Well, I've got two coming in later today. I'll get them checked in, make sure they're both okay, and we could get them over to you this evening. Is that alright?"

The elderly woman on the other end was delighted. She had been a friend of the sanctuary, and of me, for many years, and so we didn't have to carry out the usual home visits before rehoming the dogs with her—I'd been round to her place many times. It looked like the fates had smiled on us. *Peter the Peacock, you must be a good luck charm*, I said to myself as the startlingly beautiful creature walked back across the yard in front of my window, looking for all the world as if he owned the place.

Later that day, after I'd spent a good deal of time outside helping Dan with the goats, a man and a woman arrived, bringing with them the two dogs—one was a ball of long straggly fur that looked like it had been bleached blond and left with dark roots, and the other was a sweet-looking brown and white short-haired thing with a small, almost pug-like face. They both looked alert and eager, smelling the ground as they walked, their tails wagging. They were both the dearest little things. The ball of fur was carrying a red rag doll in its mouth as he trotted along, seemingly oblivious to the big change that was about to happen, while the short-haired terrier walked straight up to me and gave me a friendly sniff.

I greeted them all in the yard, conscious that my hair was not the tidiest, nor my wellies very clean. The couple didn't seem to mind. They smiled warmly and thanked me for taking in the dogs.

"You're in luck," I beamed, "assuming they're both okay, they'll be rehomed tonight. They came in at exactly the right time."

Once the formalities were over and the couple had signed the dogs over to me and left the sanctuary, they were checked over in the "emergency" extra kennel we'd had built for moments like this. They seemed like friendly dogs, and apparently they both submitted to the checks with good grace. The Yorkshire terrier had been particularly lovely, and he kept licking my hand as I stroked him when he first arrived.

As a foster carer, I knew I couldn't get too attached to each new dog, however gorgeous they were. My job with these two was to prepare them to go straight over to my friend's, and I did just that. Many animals arrive in a state of fear or trauma, or are simply stressed to be in a new place with strange people. I treat them all with the same gentleness and understanding, knowing that it didn't serve anyone if I became too fond of them.

"Now, you're both lovely, but you've got a new home to go to, and one of my motley crew will run you down there just as soon as we're happy that you're both okay," I said to them.

While the checks were taking place at the kennels, I returned to my living room and scanned the forms that all previous owners have to fill out, which ran to six pages for dogs. The documents listed all the information we might need, from questions about the dog's behavior, to their previous home life, history, and ability to play and eat and whether they were comfortable around people. There seemed to be nothing that jumped out. Each dog had lived in the one place with the elderly couple who were now too poorly to look after them, and they were both in good condition. They'd obviously been treated well. Their fur was glossy, they had no obvious marks, scars, or issues that I'd been able to see upon first inspection, and they were both a good weight. Instinctively I knew we could safely rehome them.

Just as I finished reading, the walkie-talkie buzzed. I picked it up. By now I was tired, yet I tried to keep the weariness out of my voice. It was Dan. Apparently a member of the public had reported an abandoned horse to him. He was asking if there was space for another horse on the site.

"We always make room, dearest," I said. "Go ahead and see who owns it."

It was just another busy day at the shelter.

Chapter 2

THE HAND OF FATE

Brrrrrring! Brrrrriiiiiing brrrriiiing! I reached for the phone. "Hello."

The July sunlight streamed into the living room where I was busy tidying up yet more paperwork. It was a beautiful summer morning, and I'd been up since 6 A.M., out on the land helping to feed the goats and sheep, making sure they had enough water, then breaking up the sixteen loaves of bread needed to feed the expectant birds and seagulls that sat every morning on the long line of electricity transmission lines that ran overhead and cut through the sanctuary.

"Hello, Barby, I brought two dogs to you for rehoming a month ago . . ."

It was a woman's voice, and I knew we'd spoken before. Then it all became clear.

"Yes, dear, but they went the same day. I can't help you any further on that—they're gone. You signed all the documents and there was a cooling-off period, but that's long gone, sorry dear . . ." I interjected, searching through the clutter on my desk for a form for a cat that was due to be rehomed later that day.

"Yes, thank you, you rehomed the terriers, but it wasn't the reason I was calling. I think I told you that there were four dogs that needed homes to go to . . ."

"Sorry, yes you did, do carry on," I said, flourishing the piece of paper I'd finally located. It was underneath a pile of press clippings about the sanctuary that I was collecting for my archives. The local rag, the *Bexhill Observer*, ran regular articles about the shelter, and I'd finally started to organize them for posterity. I admit I am not the most organized person in the world when it comes to pieces of paper.

"I'm ringing about the Lhasa Apso/Yorkshire terrier cross who went to live with another relative—well, it hasn't worked out, and now she needs to be rehomed as well . . ."

"Ah I see, okay, tell me everything you know and we'll see what we can do," I replied, sitting down in my comfy but ancient brown armchair.

"She's called Gabby. She's eight years old and is an absolute darling except she hasn't ever gone out of the house and isn't house-trained."

"But I don't understand, dear. You're saying she never went outside, not even to do her business?" I asked, keeping my voice calm though I felt a little agitated at the thought of this animal never having had access to the outdoors. Sometimes it is astonishing the things people do to their animals, even with the very best of intentions.

"I'm afraid so. Look, the couple loved their dogs, they never came to any harm, but for some reason they kept Gabby as a house dog. Anyway, it's Gabby that needs a new home. Her new owners simply couldn't cope with a dog that peed and pooed everywhere. They're desperately sorry, but they've decided she has to go, and I don't know where else to take her."

"Bring her here," I said without hesitation. "We don't have any room in the kennels, but I have a friend who can provide a foster home until we can rehome her permanently."

Immediately after putting the phone down, I called my friend Anne, and she got back to me straight away saying there was a lady she knew who could take her in on a temporary basis and she could come over that same day at 3 P.M.

"Well, that's another drama sorted," I said to Harry and Ben, my two pet dogs who were sitting at my feet, waiting patiently for their breakfast.

Harry was a large, well-built, blond-haired spaniel, and Ben was a black Lab. They both wagged their tails as I addressed them. They were also rescue dogs and they'd been with me for years. Harry had a long, soulful face and was quite chubby for a spaniel. He could be a little moody at times, while Ben was a flat-coated Lab with a sensitive nature who liked company and needed lots of walks, which suited me fine as most of the time I was out on the site working, and he would bound after me, tongue lolling out and tail wagging. He was an absolute darling, whereas Harry was my grumpy old man, as I liked to call him.

We agreed that they would drop Gabby off after lunch, which didn't give me much time to get everything ready for her. I buzzed Dan on my walkie-talkie and asked him to bring me the handover forms.

"And can you ask Diane if can we put a kitten somewhere? It's got an abscess, and the owner doesn't want it. They rang earlier this morning. I think there's a space on the rehoming side." It did upset me that people could give up pets at the first sign of trouble, but I had to concentrate on what was best for the animal.

"Will do."

"Oh and Dan, what I've said to Brenda is to slap the owner in the gob and take the kitten. Will that be alright?" I was joking, but everyone knew how fierce I could become when it came to pets being abandoned for, what I believed to be on this occasion, an unjustified reason.

Brenda was our highly efficient cattery administrator. She was responsible for sorting out all the details of each feline rehoming, from the initial checks and home visits to filling out the handover forms and even doing follow-up visits to check in on the cats and their new owners. A slight woman with blonde hair and piercing eyes peering out from behind her glasses, she was a very exacting kind of person, with great attention to detail, completely unlike myself! She had just retired from working in the oil industry and had fantastic organizational skills that we were able to put to good use, and she was entirely trustworthy.

"Now then, Barby, don't upset yourself, perhaps they can't afford the vet bills. Now let me get back to work."

"You're right," I conceded, "though you won't hear me admit that very often!" I cackled. I've always been a ratbag; my mother used to tell me so when I was a child. I've always had "the grumps" as she put it, and she was right. She still is. Although my spirit has been the driving force behind the sanctuary, it does get me into trouble sometimes.

A few hours later, just after lunch, the car that had appeared before with the terriers turned into the sanctuary parking lot. I watched on the CCTV camera before hurrying out to meet them all. It was the same middle-aged couple, but this time, they got out of the car without a dog in sight.

"Hello," I waved, "where's Gabby?"

"She's in the back seat, absolutely terrified. I don't think she's ever been in a car before," the man said. I nodded and went straight to the vehicle, pulling open the back door.

"Where are you, girl? Are you hiding from me? It's all okay, you're safe, it's all fine . . ." I soothed as I looked into the car.

The sight that greeted me ripped at my heart. There was a small, golden-haired dog cowering on the floor, shaking with abject terror. She was panting as if in pain and her ears were flat back against her head, showing how scared she was.

"Well, you're a beautiful girl, the lady wasn't wrong about that," I said quietly, wondering how on earth I was going to persuade this poor creature to leave the floor of the car. I sat on the seat, my legs perched out to the side, and whispered gently, telling her she was safe here with us for a few hours.

"And there's a nice woman who loves little dogs like you, and she's going to come and take care of you. Does that sound good, hey, girl?"

Gabby didn't move. She was frozen to the spot. She stared at me with her huge dark, scared eyes, and I felt my heart swell with something akin to love for her.

Now, don't you go getting carried away, Barby, this one cannot stay, you've already got two dogs, you can't take another, I said to myself.

I reached in to try and pick up Gabby, but she shrank back, never taking her eyes off mine. She didn't just look anxious—she looked traumatized. I stayed there, talking to her gently, and eventually I managed to hold her and then walk with her in my arms back into the house, her warm body against mine, shrinking into my embrace.

Harry and Ben ran to greet me, sniffing and whining a little as they smelled the unfamiliar dog in my arms. Usually they might have barked or made more of a fuss, but this time they stayed quiet, almost as if they knew how shaken up the little creature I was carrying was.

"Come here, my darling, let's put you up here on the table next to me, there's already a lovely snuggly dog bed up there. That way, Harry and Ben can't get too close.

"You are a lovely girl," I said, as Gabby's eyes followed every move I made, all the while remaining as silent as the grave.

"Going in a car is very scary to a little one like you. You did so well, and you got here. This isn't your new home but you will have one soon, I promise."

As I spoke in hushed tones, Gabby, who was still trembling, just sat there, looking at me, her big beautiful brown eyes pleading with me. Her fur was a gorgeous rich honey color, and she had soft white fur around her nose and eyes, and tufts of black on her ears and around those melting eyes. She really was an exceptionally pretty little thing.

"Don't look at me like that," I said to the dog. "You're too beautiful."

Over the next two hours, I don't think she moved once. Harry and Ben soon got bored sniffing around the base of the table where she was sitting and retreated to the rug, yawning and stretching as they settled down for a nap, but both keeping one eye open and an ear cocked for any sound from the new dog. Gabby didn't make a sound. She didn't whine or moan. She didn't move except to shift a little. She sat bolt upright, trembling still, and her eyes kept following me, never leaving mine.

"No, really, you can't look at me like that, with all your loveliness and perfectness," I stuttered, feeling an all-too-familiar surge of feeling for this helpless animal.

I sat with Gabby, chatting quietly, stroking her soft head when she eventually let me, and felt a happiness I hadn't felt in a long time. I had Ben and Harry, and I loved both of them, but, and it's very hard to describe, I knew then that I wasn't *in love* with them. They were both terrific dogs, and they'd been my companions for a while, but there was an instant connection with Gabby, a surge of protective love for her, which defied logic.

"Let's see if you can have a little walk on the floor," I said, picking up the warm bundle and putting her down. I could feel her heart beating rapidly as my arms encircled her, and I knew then that I was in trouble.

"I can't let this one go," I said to Diane, who had walked in bearing two cups of tea.

"Why's that, Barby?" She grinned, pointedly looking at

Gabby in my arms. Di worked in the cattery as a volunteer and was a kind-looking lady with wispy blonde hair framing her face. She had been with me for twenty-two years and had lived in Dad's annex since his death.

I put the dog down, holding her round her tummy, protecting her in case I had to lift her up again suddenly, as Harry wandered over for a sniff. His tail wagged furiously, and he was incredibly gentle with her.

I watched how easily Gabby had already integrated herself into our lives, and I swallowed.

"Diane, I don't think I can give this one up, I really can't. It's weird but she feels like mine, it's fate that she's here at all. She wasn't meant to be with that relative of the old couple. She's here, and she's just so lovely."

Diane raised one eyebrow. It was her stern look, and I saw it often, though I always gave as good as I got in return.

"Well, you have to make your mind up. You've got that lady driving over here and you don't want her to waste her time if you really feel you can't live without Gabby . . ."

I picked up the dog again. Gabby turned her delightful face to mine and licked me. It felt like a sign. I made my decision. I reached for the telephone, punching in the numbers at lightning speed. I checked the clock. It was 3:45 P.M. The woman was late. Perhaps she wasn't coming? As I thought that, my heart responded with a bolt of pure adrenaline mixed with joy—oh dear, I was in trouble. I knew I'd fallen for Gabby, and so I hoped the woman hadn't got lost. I didn't want her to have a wasted journey.

If I could just get hold of Anne, she could call the woman on her cell phone.

"Anne, thank goodness you're there. I have some news." My friend cut me off. "Barby, so sorry, but the fosterer can't come today. She got lost and had to turn back. Could she come back tomorrow?"

Again, it felt like the hand of fate had intervened.

"Anne, I'm sorry, but I'm ringing you to say that we've already found a home for Gabby, so would you please ring the foster carer and say we're awfully sorry, but there's no need for her to come?"

"No problem at all, I'll let her know. Speak soon, Barby."

"Thank you, dear, thank you," I said as I put the phone down, my heart lifting with joy.

Turning to Gabby, I pulled her gently in to me. Her shakes had stopped, but she was still very quiet, making only the occasional snuffling sound.

"I told Anne you've been rehomed, but I didn't tell her it's with me. You're my dog now, darling one. Welcome to your new home."

Chapter 3

LITTLE PRISONER

When a dog is introduced into a household that already has dogs, it is always best to keep the newcomer separate for a few days until they all get used to each other. It has to be a gradual process of introduction as dogs are territorial creatures and are liable to turn on a new animal if it isn't integrated properly. Fortunately I had no real worries with Harry and Ben. Harry could be quite grumpy and a bit of a sulker, adorable though he was, but that was about as nasty as he got. Ben would probably lick Gabby to death, but I didn't want to take any chances. Also, Gabby was clearly in such a state, I didn't want to stress her any further.

I looked around for the baby gate I'd used in the past, but couldn't see the damn thing anywhere.

"Dan, where's that baby gate gone? I can't find it. I must be getting muddled in my old age," I said down the walkie-talkie, knowing full well that my memory was still excellent.

There were so many people traipsing in and out of my

rooms day in, day out that things got put in awkward places or moved to entirely new places, which was very frustrating.

Dan's voice crackled back at me. "I last saw it in the office. Look there."

"Thank you, dear," I said, walking into the small room to the side that doubled as an office to the right of the front door, tucked away behind the kitchen. In the room was a desk, piles of paperwork, a rather sorry-looking computer, and— the baby gate.

"There you are. You were hiding from me!" I chuckled to myself, bringing it through to my bedroom. My bathroom led directly from there, and it made the perfect little den to put Gabby in to give her time to settle in and get used to her new surroundings. I put a cozy dog basket filled with snuggly blankets and cushions into the floor space between the shower and the sink, making sure there was a blanket she'd already sat on so she could smell her own distinctive doggy smell. That would give her some measure of reassurance, at least. I placed several squashy toys, a soft fox toy, and a bowl for water in there, too, as well as some newspaper and a litter tray.

"There you go, girl, a palace fit for a princess. Now, there's no need to cry, you're safe here with me, poor Gabby."

The dog had started making the smallest moaning sound, barely a whisper, but it signaled her distress. The noise was low and deeply sad, like a baby left for hours with no one to hear them cry. I felt that noise as a physical sensation, my heart heavy for her. She was suffering, and all I could do was stay with her, stroke her lovely head, and reassure her over and over again.

Gabby's breeding would also have been a factor in her shrinking away from a new owner. The Lhasa Apso in her would be suspicious of strangers, and I knew I would have to earn her trust. The Yorkshire terrier part of her, which was very evident around the shape of her face, would be happy to be warm and coddled in the blankets. It would make her harder to house-train, as Yorkie crosses sometimes inherit a willfulness or stubbornness. I would need time, and lots of patience, to figure out which of the breed characteristics were uppermost in Gabby's constitution and personality.

At the moment, she seemed relatively calm, which was a blessing. Gabby huddled down into the blankets, and I sat there, uttering soft words, telling her she was home now and she would have a lovely new life with lots of outdoors play.

"You won't believe the land outside. When I show you the animals, with all their wonderful noises and smells, you will be in heaven. There are fields and grass, and there's mud to roll in, and lots of real foxes to sniff. We'll go for a walk in the fields together, and I'll tell you all about the horses and the donkeys, the ponies and the goats that live here. I'll introduce you to the chickens and hens, but I'd stay away from the geese if I were you, they can get very territorial and you're only a little thing."

As I was speaking, Gabby didn't take her eyes off me. Soft, big brown eyes framed by black eyelashes, and that irresistible golden fur with splashes of white. Her eyes were huge puddles of confusion and sadness. I felt her pain as if we were somehow connected, and so I stayed sitting beside her, crooning to her into the evening.

Harry and Ben had sat on the other side of the baby gate, their heads cocked to one side, wondering, no doubt, what on earth was going on. Normally when dogs were left with us, they went straight to the kennels and didn't come into the house. This new creature coming in and joining us was a new experience for them, and they were just as confused, though clearly excited and happy to see her. Their tails wagged every time Gabby sniffed, but eventually, as Gabby remained lying there staring up at me, they lost interest and wandered off.

I stepped back over the gate, catching sight of myself in the bathroom mirror as I went. My ash blonde hair, streaked with the beginnings of gray, was tied back in a practical pony-tail. Gone were the glorious days when I'd sculpt my blonde tresses into a beehive. My T-shirt had the logo of the sanctuary charity on it, and I wore a pair of utilitarian work trousers, ones I could get dirty without a care in the world. Since we became a charity I'd proudly printed T-shirts and fleece sweatshirts with our logo on them, which would be sold at the forthcoming Open Day and were already on sale in our new shop in Bexhill. I brushed back a stray hair and grinned at myself. *Not model material now, are you, Barby? But then again the animals don't mind what I look like, so who cares?* I chuckled as I left, walking into the kitchen where my two dogs greeted me as if I'd been away for years. I guessed that they might be feeling a little neglected.

"You silly boys. I'm here now to feed you, and we've all

got to look after beautiful Gabby. She needs space and quiet to settle in, and lots of love, but we can give her that, can't we, gorgeous boys?"

Ben had come up, licked my hand, and indicated he wanted his tummy rubbed. I obliged before going to the cupboard and taking out the tins of the food they liked and started hunting for the can opener.

That night, Harry and Ben flopped down with huge great sighs onto my bed, and I idly patted their heads as I talked to Gabby, who was lying only feet away from us in the bathroom, explaining to her that we were all going to sleep, and she had nothing to worry about when it got dark. She made no sound in response. Not a murmur.

As I laid back, I could hear her snuffled breathing, but there was no moaning or crying for her previous owners, nor any barking to signal her frustration at being kept "prisoner" in the bathroom; in fact, there was still no sound from her at all. All night I lay there, Harry and Ben fast asleep slumped over me, listening for the little dog, worrying about her, and forcing myself not to get out of bed and go in there with her. I had never known a dog who stayed completely silent like Gabby. I must've dropped off eventually, as I awoke to sunlight streaming through the room through the window at the end of my bed, and Harry licking my face.

"Get off me, daft animal. I know you like giving me kisses. . . . That's enough, Harry. Morning, Ben, don't you join in as well!" I cried, as Ben loped up to "help" my spaniel give me a morning wash.

"Come on, we've got to check on that little scrap in the

bathroom. Get off me, you two." I laughed, heaved myself off the bed, and climbed over the gate.

Gabby was still silent, but I could tell she'd had a difficult night, as the stench from her bed was hard to ignore.

"Oh dear, Gabby darling, you've had a few accidents in there, haven't you, girl? When you get settled, the first thing you're going to learn is how to do your business outside in the fields like Harry and Ben."

I chatted away, trying not to gag from the smell. Gabby had both pooed and peed into her bedding. She had ignored the newspaper and litter tray, which made me think that either she'd never used one before, or she was so unsettled that she just couldn't find the courage to get out of her bed. I knew she couldn't help it. I suspected that she'd never used a litter tray before, but that was okay—we could soon teach her that. I wouldn't have dreamt of shouting at Gabby. She didn't know what she was doing.

"We'll have to give you a nice shower to make you clean again, and I think this bedding will have to be thrown out. Oh dear, poor Gabby, you must be in a state, my darling." Gabby let me wash her down without a peep from her.

She made no sound at all and every now and then she started trembling, so I scooped her into my arms and rocked her like a baby until she stopped. I did wonder how the previous owners had managed with a dog who wasn't house-trained. The fact that she was kept as a house pet made me feel that she really had been a little prisoner, a prisoner of their love perhaps, but regardless, it was a strange way to treat a dog. I'd never known a dog kept just as a house pet. Some

cats are fine with that, but a dog needs fresh air, lots of space
to run about, and walks with their owner that cement the
human–animal bond. None of this appeared to have taken
place, and frankly it puzzled me, and made me feel terribly sad.
I didn't for a moment think that the elderly couple had delib-
erately mistreated her. Perhaps they became too infirm to train
her or even to go outside themselves. Perhaps Gabby herself
had not wanted to go out. The hardest part was that I would
never know the truth. The couple had both been taken into
a nursing home, and so I didn't feel I could ring up and find
out any more about what had taken place.

"Gabby darling, I'm going to bring you some breakfast,
you must be hungry."

Gabby, now clean but still a bit soggy, sat down on her
new bedding and just stared back up at me. I could've wept.
She looked so serious, yet already I could tell that she was
alert and intelligent. Gabby took everything in, and looked to
me like she was thinking and processing all the new people,
animals, and places she'd experienced so suddenly in the past
twenty-four hours.

"Come on, here's some biscuits and some food. Try and eat
up, there's a good girl. That will help make you feel better."

I was heartened to see Gabby start to eat, though she only
ate a little.

"Better than nothing. We'll try again later," I said to her
kindly, taking the food bowl and leaving her the biscuits and
some water.

The rest of the day was spent checking on Gabby every
ten minutes. If I had to head out to the farm animals, or to

go and meet someone dropping off a cat for rehoming, or people wanted to look at the dogs for potential rehoming, I made sure somebody went in and checked she was okay. All the time Gabby sat in that bathroom, Harry stayed close almost as if he was guarding her. It was only Ben who followed me around the sanctuary that day.

"You've found your protector there, girl," I said fondly when I came in to check on Gabby at lunchtime, rubbing Harry's long ears and ruffling his wavy fur. Both dogs looked up at me, and call it a sixth sense, but in that moment I had a feeling that she would be fine.

Chapter 4

HOUSE ARREST

All dogs are descended from wolves. They are predators beneath the cozy domesticity; the training and behaviors that have evolved are a result of living in close contact with humans. When confronted with cuddly toys created to look like prey—small rabbits, foxes, and cats, for example—most dogs instantly connect with their natural instincts, each toy becoming an echo of the animals' wild nature, and they pounce. They chew them, roll with them, gnaw them, and snarl—becoming wolflike for the duration of their play, evoking an uncomplicated relationship with smaller creatures, that of hunter and hunted.

Over the years I've seen my soppy, lovable hounds rip their cuddly toys to bits after stalking them, pouncing and making them their prey. It's a glorious throwback to their elemental natures. They were once wild beasts and such behavior is proof that the seed of this drive stayed within them through centuries of breeding. Warding off intruders or strangers to the pack is also an inbuilt reaction, an ancient impulse that serves to protect the group through growling, barking, and hackles rising. Yet over the following two days, while Gabby was still in the process of being integrated into our home, she remained silent. None of the normal, natural impulses of barking or playing with the toys were evident. Every time I came back inside to check up on her, she was sitting almost in the position I'd left her in on her bed, her food barely touched and her litter tray unused.

It was a little past midday two days after she arrived and I decided I needed to spend some more time with Gabby, who we all joked was under "house arrest."

"Now then, girl, we need to see you settling in a bit. How about if I come in there with you and try and comfort you, eh?" I said, climbing over the gate.

Gabby looked up at me, and her tail moved a centimeter or so to each side.

"You're wagging your tail at me. Good girl, see, we're getting there, aren't we?"

I picked up the fox. It was made of orange and white felt. One of the ears had been chewed, but it was still intact. I stood up and shook the toy at her gently, sliding it along the floor and making it jump a little. Gabby stared at it for a while, then turned her adorable face to mine. Was it my imagination, or was she looking confused?

"Okay, let's try this," I said, "desperate times call for desperate measures . . ." and I held the fox up to my mouth and made gnashing noises, trying to show her what a dog would normally do with this type of toy. I slumped down onto the floor and pretended to roll over before I burst out laughing.

"Still nothing?" I said when my chuckles had subsided. Again, Gabby looked back up at me with those beautiful, sad-looking eyes, none of my attempts seemingly registering with her. Though I felt a little silly playing at being a dog, I did it because something had occurred to me, but I still needed more proof.

Just then, there was a loud knock at the front door. Both Harry and Ben shot up, Ben, presumably from his place lounging on the front room rug, and Harry from his position next to the baby gate, guarding Gabby, and they both ran down the corridor, barking as they went. I turned my head to see Gabby's reaction. Nothing, yet again.

"Don't worry, girl, it's probably someone to see the rehoming cats. I'll be back in a minute."

I made my way to the door, my mind momentarily distracted from my thoughts about Gabby and her strange lack of doggie behavior.

"Yes, dear, can I help you?" I said as I opened the door. Before the woman standing in front of me could say anything, a chicken ran inside, squawking as she went.

"Oh that's Henrietta, don't mind her, she's a house chicken, she lives here," I said casually, as if this was the most normal thing in the world.

The woman, a nice-looking lady with shoulder-length blonde hair and an open smile, laughed, then said, "Hello, I'm Christine. I've been volunteering for a while, but I don't think I've ever properly introduced myself."

Normally I don't warm to people straight away, but with Christine it was different. I'd seen her around the site and said hello before, so I knew who she was and that she was an excellent worker. I didn't usually get much time to socialize, but I knew from her gentle ways and calm, down-to-earth approach that we would get on like a house on fire. She had a sunny smile and a kind look about her. She must have been in her late forties or early fifties, but she seemed younger.

"You're very welcome, my dear. I'm Barby. It's very nice to meet you. You're working at the kennels, I seem to recall?"

"Yes, I am, it's great. So different to my work, it gives me a bit of breathing space, a bit of sanity!" She laughed.

"What do you do, dear?" I asked. "And come in, don't stand there on the doormat."

Christine followed me inside. "Actually I'm an end-of-life nurse. I was a 'normal' nurse for years at the Conquest Hospital in Hastings but then transferred to a place in Bexhill, where I care for people with limited time left. It's very rewarding work, but it can be draining, and that's where your sanctuary comes in. I can come up here, look after the dogs that come in, and forget my worries." She shrugged, giving me a warm smile.

At that moment, Harry, who had gone back to sit outside Gabby's nest, walked back into the living room. Christine was perched on the arm of the sofa, and she immediately bent down to stroke him, her face softening as she petted him. It was obvious she was dog-mad. My kind of woman. I could already see there was something special about her. Call it intuition, but I knew we would become firm friends.

Just then Henrietta strutted in and, flapping her tawny

wings, ascended in a rather higgledy-piggledy fashion up onto the back of the sofa.

"Henrietta, have some manners!" I fumed in mock horror. "We have a guest. Don't mind that silly hen. She comes in most afternoons to settle down and wait for the football to come on the telly."

Christine looked back at me, her face a picture of amusement and confusion.

"Henrietta loves Manchester United," I sighed. My life at the sanctuary really was extraordinary. You couldn't make this up. "And whenever they play she jumps up and down each time they score. It's the truth. She really loves them and has done for the whole of the three years she's been with us. The staff has taken to calling her David Peckham . . ." I grinned, "and together they got her a Man U scarf to wear. Ridiculous, really, but there you go . . ."

"Well, I've never heard of a football-loving chicken," beamed Christine, "but she certainly looks like she's ready for action."

We both looked round at the daft bird. She looked back at us from her position on my settee with absolute confidence.

"I'd better get back, or they'll wonder where I've gone. Thanks for the chat and lovely to meet you, Barby," Christine said, getting up and heading for the front door.

"Likewise, dear, come back for a cuppa anytime," I replied, finding myself smiling with that particular happiness that comes of making a new friend.

Later that day, I was sitting alone in my living room, pondering the situation with Gabby. She was still so quiet that at times I forgot she was in the next room. Henrietta was sitting on the back of the sofa, moving her head now and then in that jerky fashion, her beady eyes blinking. Gabby was a puzzle I needed to crack. Just then the phone rang.

"Hello, can I help you?"

"Yes, hello, I'm sorry to bother you but I have four chickens who need to be rehomed. I've been diagnosed with an illness and can't keep them anymore. Could you take them?" The woman's voice was filled with sadness. People get so attached to their animals—they become part of the family, whatever breed or species they are.

"Yes, dear, we can take them. In fact I know a man who is looking for some more chickens, the fox got his last lot, so as long as he can reassure me that he's fixed their overnight run, I can send them his way."

"Oh that's such a relief. Thank you," she replied.

"Could you bring them in within the next hour?" I asked, knowing that the man who wanted chickens could get here quickly, and we could successfully rehome them all today. It was all agreed.

When I put the phone down, Henrietta was staring at me with such a piercing look that I laughed.

"Don't worry, Hen, I won't be rehoming you. No one would take you." My sense of humor was rather wicked at the best of times.

Di wandered in, still wearing her muddy wellies. She was wearing a fleece jacket that had seen better days and a pair of rather mucky trousers.

"Barby, I've got to go to the vet. We have a cat with a bad eye, and I wanted to let you know."

"Thank you, dear. I'll put that in my book, now where is it?" I said, searching under the piles of papers, books, and general admin clutter that surrounded me.

"There it is," I said at last, brandishing it. "Now I just need a pen . . ."

"Barby, the volunteers want to come in for a cup of tea. Is it okay to let them?" asked Di hesitantly.

"Yes, as long as they bloody well behave," I retorted, a grin on my face. "I mean it—last week one of them had an argument and stormed out. I don't want any of that nonsense while I'm here." I grumbled, finally putting my hands on my pen.

"Right, dear, now tell me about the cat . . ."

I recorded every vet visit in a big book with every animal's name and their ailment. It was to keep track of the bills and the animals' welfare. Our monthly vets' bills were eye-watering, running into the thousands of pounds, so I had to keep a very close eye on things.

At that point, a troupe of people wandered in, most having removed their dirty wellies at the front door.

"Do you want tea, Barby?" called one of them, a nice lad called William who was a regular at the sanctuary. He hadn't been with us for long, but he was extremely intelligent and could be relied upon to find solutions to most issues that arose. He was a tall fellow with a beard and a pleasant smile, and I had also warmed to him from the first day he arrived.

"No, thank you, William. I need to make a call about some chickens."

After I'd logged the cat in the vet book, I dug out the number of the man who wanted some replacement fowl. His phone rang, and eventually he picked up.

"Hello dear, it's Barby. Did you still want some chickens?" was all I said.

Within minutes it was all sorted. He would come in the next hour to collect them once they'd arrived from the ill lady. Sometimes, things just clicked into place here. We didn't need to fill out forms or process the arrival or departure of the birds as they didn't need to be officially registered, so the handovers were usually smooth and quick, though I could tell from the woman's voice earlier that she would be devastated to say good-bye to her "girls."

Finally the volunteers all finished their teas and coffees and departed. Eight of them had come in for a break, and their ages ranged from early teens right through to several women in their seventies. A love of animals cuts across all ages, races, and backgrounds of people. We had some fantastically wealthy supporters, who were more than happy to roll up their designer sleeves, put on their expensive wellies, and help muck out the pigs. We had people who would otherwise be unemployable, who had mental health issues, or who had suffered addiction or other health problems who found solace working with the animals. We had everyone, from housewives and hardworking women, to former company CEOs and even a few ladies-who-lunch, all of them passionate about helping animals. At the sanctuary, we didn't care where you came from, who you thought you were, or what your political views were. If you could wash out a poorly cat's soiled bedding, clean out the kennels, walk the dogs through the surrounding fields, and help feed the sheep, goats, pigs, and horses, then you fitted right in.

The living room was finally empty, apart from me and Ben, who I stroked absentmindedly. Henrietta had disappeared as soon as the hordes descended upon us. I took the chance to visit Gabby again, this time with some more biscuits and a chew as a treat.

My heart sank when I saw her, because she was still sitting there and didn't appear to have explored her little area at all, though at least she had company in the form of Harry who, as ever, was guarding her "cage."

"Good boy, Harry. You're a brilliant guard dog. Gabby won't come to any harm with you around," I said softly, climbing over the gate and tickling Harry's ears as I went. It was important not to neglect my other dogs while I was so focused on this beautiful new wee thing.

This time Gabby got up slowly and stepped forward to sniff my hand. She started to lick it, and I beamed with pleasure.

"Good girl! That's more like it. Have you seen Harry doing that? Is that why you now know how to make friends in a doggy way?" I said, as much to myself as to her.

My thoughts had crystallized, and I knew now what was happening and why Gabby was as she was.

"Here you go, girl, a chew to munch on." I dropped the edible stick beside her, but Gabby didn't even look at it. She ignored it as if she'd never seen one before. It didn't surprise me; in fact, it only served to reinforce what I was already thinking.

I threw another stick over the gate to Harry, who devoured it almost as soon as it hit the carpet.

"Look, see Gabby. That's how Harry eats his chew. Why don't you give it a go?"

Gabby turned those liquid brown eyes to me, and this time I was certain—it was a look of utter confusion.

"Don't worry, poppet, I know what's going on here. We'll sort you out in no time. Just keep looking at Harry, he'll show you the way . . ."

At that point, Ben ambled in, and at the sight of Harry sitting there, having finished his chew, he pounced, and the two of them started to roll about on the floor, play-fighting.

I sat and watched Gabby as they tussled, making mock growling noises and panting as they rolled, then leapt up, nibbled each other, and pretended to be in fierce combat.

Gabby just continued to sit there, her head moving from side to side as she watched them. She didn't seem alarmed by their fighting—she must've witnessed play fighting with the dogs she'd grown up with—but she made no attempt to try and join in or play herself.

Dan's voice called from the kitchen.

"Barby, you there?"

"I'm with Gabby," I shouted back.

Dan's footsteps announced him, and then his head poked round the bedroom door.

"Have you got a minute? I need to tell you about a horse someone has reported as being abandoned . . ."

"In a minute, Dan, just watch this," I said, looking back at the sight of my two dogs romping joyously in the room while Gabby sat there, silent as the grave, watching them without a flicker of recognition.

"I've worked it out. Gabby doesn't know how to bark. She doesn't know how to play or how to do her business outside. In short, she doesn't know how to be a dog."

Chapter 5

WORK BEGINS

O ne of the things I'd noticed about Gabby, despite her reluctance to join in with doggie behaviors, was how inquisitive she was. Often, I'd catch her watching Harry and Ben, her eyes following them around the room, taking in everything they did. I could tell even just from that that she was probably a bright, curious animal—I just hadn't managed to coax out her true spirit yet.

Gabby spent four days behind the baby gate, a little longer than I would have liked, but as she was so quiet I wanted to go at her pace. I didn't want to unsettle her further by taking her out too soon. I was worried it would set her back. Over those four days she had made some progress. She'd started to wag her tail and greet me when I arrived, though she had always stayed in her sitting position. She still ignored the toys, and hadn't yet made a single sound, but I decided it was time to bring her out and let her join the household, especially as I was now reassured that my two other dogs, Harry and Ben, weren't a threat to her.

If anything, it was exactly the reverse situation. Harry seemed besotted by Gabby, and she was so beautiful, I couldn't blame him. Ben had grown bored of the lack of response from her and wandered in and out of the bedroom to sniff at the baby gate only occasionally.

The day came for the ceremonial taking down of the gate.

"Come on, Ben, oh look, there's Harry, on sentry duty," I smiled as we walked into the bedroom.

"Gabby, my darling, we're going to bring you into the living room today so you can start to settle in and make this house your new home. We will look after you and stay with you all the time, so you don't need to worry . . ." I soothed, turning the screw that bolted the gate to the wall. Once the tension had been released, the gate collapsed against me, and I strode back to the office to return it, first making sure the bathroom door was closed behind me.

"Diane, come and see this. We're letting Gabby out today."

"She'll be alright, won't she?" Di quizzed, cocking her head to one side. She was making herself a cup of tea in the kitchen.

"Well, we can't keep her locked up behind there forever," I retorted, "she has to come out sooner rather than later, so let's just get on with it."

Di nodded. "You know best, Barby," she replied, following me into my bedroom with a steaming hot cuppa in her hand.

I had a double bed in there covered in blankets that the dogs slept on, and various cupboards and shelves for my things. It wasn't glamorous, but it all served a purpose. I have always been a practical person, preferring clothes to keep me warm and dry rather than make me look like a supermodel, and that translated to everything else in my life. My home would never appear in a glossy magazine, but it suited me just fine. My living room was my headquarters. It was the heart of the sanctuary and where I took all the phone calls and sorted through paperwork. It also housed my growing collection of meerkat dolls.

I've always been a collector. As a young woman I collected ashtrays even though I've never smoked. I grew bored of that and started on wind chimes, of which I now have hundreds, and then I switched to the meerkats. I had an all-consuming drive to possess every fluffy toy made by a certain insurance comparison website. Something about them tickled me and made me smile, and that was a good enough reason for me to keep them.

I had meerkats of all descriptions—soft, cuddly ones, solid stone ones in the sunroom, plastic ones, boxed ones—and many of them were collector's items. It was another of my little eccentricities, and every birthday I'd receive a whole new set of them from all those who knew me well. The collection had spilled across the set of cabinets that framed my armchair area, down onto the nearby cupboards and was already encroaching onto the table that sat next to my chair that usually housed the dog beds for Harry and Ben.

"Right now, Gabby, I'm going to pick you up and take you into the front room and sit you by the fire, won't that be lovely, eh girl? Now I know it's July still, and the fire won't actually be lit, but we won't worry about that. This is just to practice for the winter when you can curl up all cozy in front of it and enjoy the snuggly rug there . . ."

As I talked in a calm, quiet voice, Gabby stirred, and she let me pick her up and carry her. I could feel her warm belly against me, and this time, I was heartened to feel her heart thumping with slow regularity. She wasn't stressed by this new turn of events. That had to be a good thing. Gabby turned her sweet face up to mine. The soft white hairs around her nose and chin tickled me as she gazed into my eyes, never once looking away.

"No wonder I fell for you, you're such a little darling, such a good girl . . ." I carried on reassuring her, delighted that this was proving easier than I expected. Gabby licked my nose, and I felt a moment of pure joy and love for this little creature with her warm soft fur and her bright soulful eyes.

At that moment my instincts kicked in, and I realized that putting her down away from me might trigger separation anxiety. I'd worked hard, spending lots of time with Gabby behind the baby gate to help her to attach to me so that she could relax and get used to her new space. I knew she would feel lost if I "abandoned" her by placing her at the other end of the room.

"You're coming to sit with me, Gabby. We'll have a nice cuddle here on my armchair."

All the time, as I spoke and sat down gently in my chair, Harry and Ben were at my heels. Harry sat, his tail wagging, making a kind of whining noise I recognized as a gentle way of marking his territory. He loved Gabby, too, and there was no doubt he saw the dog as his as much as mine. I couldn't fault him for his loyalty. Over the preceding four days he'd only left Gabby's side to do his business outdoors and eat his dinner. He'd stayed with her all that time.

"Thank you, Harry, you've done a wonderful job of guarding Gabby. Now perhaps we can all concentrate on showing this little one how to actually be a dog!"

Harry must've heard the ring of truth in my voice, because he barked a small responsive bark.

"See Gabby, that's how a dog barks. One day you'll be able to do that, too."

Gabby made no sound in reply; she simply stared back into my eyes. All of a sudden I felt emotional, and tears welled up. Something about the innocence of this dog made me feel protective, almost like a mother caring for a very young baby. Gabby would need to be trained to become a dog, rather like a child is shown how to be an adult, how to talk, walk, cuddle, and eat. I would have to guide Gabby through each new way of behaving, and somehow I knew I would have Harry's help, and I wondered as well if Gabby knew she had a helper already in hand. There was clearly a connection between the two dogs, made from the first moment she entered the house. It was a special thing to witness two animals in agreement, with a bond like this, and I felt happy that not only would Gabby have a human guide, she would have the most important thing of all: a doggie guide to help her become her true self.

After sitting with Gabby for much of the morning, it was time for me to get up and go to meet some people at the gate who wanted to rehome two cats. Reluctantly, I placed Gabby down on the rug, next to Harry who had moved over there, lying down with his face on his paws but never taking his eyes off his charge.

"Now, Harry, I want you to take care of Gabby while I'm gone. I'll only be half an hour or so." I had thought about taking her with me, carrying her in my arms, but I didn't want to overwhelm her with new people, new smells, and new noises all at once. It was better she stayed indoors but I hated leaving her, even for such a short time. I knew that Gabby might not like my going, that she might construe it as being abandoned again. As I left, I buzzed Diane on the walkie-talkie asking her to drop what she was doing and come straight over to sit with Gabby until my return.

I met the people, a man and a woman from the local area, and took them over to the cattery, where I gave them a short tour before handing them over to Di and a couple of volunteers who were more than capable of handling the initial rehoming requests. Anyone wanting to rehome a pet is shown around the cattery or kennels so that they can decide if any of the cats or dogs look suitable for them. If an animal is picked, there is a process to follow before it can be taken home. We need to make sure that the animal is being offered a permanent and loving home, and if I'm not satisfied that this is going to happen, I refuse the rehoming request without hesitation.

There are forms that have to be filled in by the prospective owners about the suitability of their new home. These are handed to Brenda for her to check over. If everything looks okay, she then arranges a home visit to make sure the abode is suitable for the animal. The chosen animal is also checked over by the vet, making sure they have been spayed or neutered, and any medications are explained to the prospective owners. This whole process takes a couple of weeks, and it also gives people time to think, so that any decisions they make are the right ones. It's always joyous to see a cat or a dog taken off with excited new owners. Our checks are so thorough that rarely do we have any problems with new owners.

I headed back, keen to see how Gabby had coped with my absence. She was curled up on the rug with Harry lying next to her, so close he was almost touching her. Di sat beside her, watching her every move. My heart melted yet again at the sight of them. Where Harry was a cool blond, Gabby was the color of runny honey with those patches of startling white that made her so pretty. As I walked in, she looked up, and her tail wagged more markedly this time. I clapped my hands with delight.

"We'll make a dog of you yet," I said.

"There you are," said Di. "She's been a poppet, though she started trembling when you left and wouldn't settle. She didn't moan, but then she doesn't seem to make a sound at all, so I don't think that's an indication that she was okay. The poor little thing paced round and round on the rug. I almost called you to come back."

"Poor Gabby," I said, crouching down beside her and stroking her still-shaking body. She looked up at me, her eyes like saucers, and filled with sadness and longing, and I almost wept thinking of her distress, and the fact she still couldn't articulate it in a doggie way.

Harry looked up at me as if to say "I've got this, Mum," and laid back down, sniffing gently at Gabby's ears and prodding her with his nose as if to tell her, "Mummy's here." I stayed kneeling on the rug next to them and Gabby sat up. I held out my arms, and she walked into them. Things were definitely moving in the right direction.

"I've never seen anything like it before," I said to Keith, my friend and darts partner, as we sat drinking our evening cuppas together. Keith, who had a stocky build, had a kind face and brown hair. He was a gentle, reserved man who did building jobs around the site. He was currently rebuilding the cattery in time for the next lot of visitors, and after work some evenings he'd come over and we'd practice darts in my house using a board I'd had fitted at the end of the corridor that linked my bedroom and the main living area. He'd join me for a quick drink and a chat afterward before heading home.

"This dog doesn't know how to be a dog. It's most unusual. In all my years running this sanctuary, I don't think I've ever seen another case like it," I said, stirring my tea.

Most evenings I watched the news or the soap opera *Emmerdale* unless Keith was popping in. Everyone knew not to disturb me during my program, or they'd get a piece of my mind, so I was left to myself to wind down and enjoy taking my mind off the daily business of the sanctuary.

Gabby was sleeping on my lap, where she'd spent most of the day. Getting to the loo was tricky—she stared at me with such yearning in her eyes when I moved to get up that I almost gave up trying at times.

The dog was still not using her litter tray and so I'd put down newspaper everywhere to catch her accidents. There had been several during the day, and even though it wasn't pleasant to find dog poo in the living room, I would never have dared shout at her or tell her off in any way. It was obvious she didn't know any better. I'd warned the staff to be careful about where they trod in the house, and that was all I could do until I could help Gabby do her business outside.

"She's a lovely dog, though," replied Keith, sipping his tea.

"She's gorgeous, look at her, she'd get away with murder with a face like that."

We both peered at her. Gabby just stared back, looking between us with that puzzled expression that I now knew so well. I sighed. "She looks stunned, I think. It's been very overwhelming for her. I think going in the car for the first time, then being outside, albeit briefly, and then being placed in a new home with lots of new scents and noises from the animals—well, it's overloaded her. She went into shock, there's no other way to describe it. I've seen the same look on the face of the horses that are caught and brought here, especially when they've been left to run wild."

Keith nodded again. "You'll teach her, though, won't you?" he asked, though it was more a statement of fact than a question.

"I will do my very best," I replied, looking down at the dog. I stroked her soft back and rubbed her under her ears. She moved her head and looked up at me, sniffing my hand and giving it an exploratory lick.

"I know it was the right decision to keep her and not place her with a foster carer. She would've been disturbed by yet another exposure to being outside, another car journey, another person and place to get used to and another home after that. I really think it would have broken her. She's such a quiet sensitive thing that I know it would have been almost impossible to have recovered from that."

"And you adore her . . ." Keith said pointedly, though smiling at me in his kind way.

"And I fell in love with her," I admitted. It was pointless denying it. I have always carried my feelings on my face, never able to hide my emotions. My emotions flow, up and down, from upset to rage to heartbroken in a single day. I am a passionate woman. I love animals to the point that I value their lives more than my own. I hate injustice or cruelty, and it shows on my face, just as much as the love I feel always does. It was obvious to everyone around me that I had already developed a deep connection with this dog, one that transcended carer and hound. It was like meeting an old friend at last, or a feeling that Gabby had always been with me, although in reality she'd only been here for four short days.

"She's mine," I said simply, "and from the minute I saw her cowering in that car, I knew she was mine."

She just needed time, but I had a feeling that teaching her how to be a dog was going to be harder than I initially thought, even though we'd made some small steps forward. After all, I was going to have to reverse eight years of her life. It is the story of animal fostering, and it is frustrating at times. One just has to work out a way to love each animal back to their own spirits and selves, digging out their own unique personalities and foibles.

"It's what I do, but I have to say that Gabby, for all her

beauty, is probably the biggest challenge I've ever faced," I said, looking at the little scrap huddled next to me.

And with that, we both sipped our tea in silence, pondering the journey that lay before me as the summer evening drew in. When Keith left, I switched on the television, the room becoming brighter as the light faded over the outlying fields and enclosures. The animal noises that surrounded me switched to nighttime mode: the sheep started baaa-ing for their supper, the horses whinnied in the back fields. birds sang for the last time of the day as they settled down, calling out their territories to their feathered rivals, while the roosters crowed and the hens clucked in that gentle evening way as they, too, acknowledged the darkness falling.

Chapter 6

HARRY TO THE RESCUE

"That's it, Gabby, go on, girl, you're almost there . . ."
I stood in the living room doorway, willing her to take the extra step forward that would send her through the dog door and out into the big, wide world.

"You're almost there, almost touching it. . . . Oh, never mind, gorgeous girl, never mind."

I tried to keep my voice steady as Gabby backed off away from the exit, her nerves failing her yet again, but I knew my exasperation was showing. Gabby had been with us for just over two weeks, and she still hadn't made it outside, even though she could see the other dogs going in and out of the house. Her confidence had grown in that time, there was no doubt about that, and the fact that she would even sniff at the exit showed me that she was thinking about going through it, but despite this I was feeling frustrated. I didn't want to push her; if I took her outside to try and acclimatize her in a short, sharp way, I knew it would put her progress back and possibly traumatize her again. With this little dog I knew I had to go slowly.

"Never mind, Gabby, we can try again later," I sighed, watching her trot back to the front room.

Earlier, I had tried holding a dish of food outside to see if she could be coaxed through by the tantalizing smell of her dinner, but even that hadn't worked. It was tempting to try and hold her, to physically ease her through the door, but even that felt like it was rushing her.

"You'll get there. One day, you'll get up, stretch, yawn, then head out to do your business without even thinking about it," I said, perhaps more in hope than belief.

I had to see today's attempt as a small victory. After all, she had got as far as sniffing the inside edge of the opening, which sat to the right of my front door and was usually covered with a blanket to keep out drafts.

There was no need for the blanket this evening. It was a balmy day in early August and less than a week away from our Open Day. Our Summer Bazaar, or Open Day, as we usually referred to it, was the highlight of our year's fund-raising events, and the one we all enjoyed the most because of the sunshine. It always brought out the best in people.

As usual I was up to my neck in things to organize, from booking and organizing the booths to making sure the site was safe and up to scratch with health and safety regulations. Despite the long list of everything I had to do, my work with Gabby was foremost on my mind.

Over the two weeks she'd been with me, I had started encouraging Gabby to try and use the dog door every hour or so, but she had resisted each and every time, and I could see now that it was probably best to let her find her own way to it.

What encouraged me the most was her growing relationship with Harry. He was a very handsome boy with his thick, light-colored fur, long floppy ears, and dark eyes, but he could also be a devil. When he first arrived at the sanctuary a couple of years earlier, he bit everything and everyone he could. I couldn't let him loose in the yard or round the site as he would chase the chickens, geese, and cats. He had been a nightmare! Something about him stuck, though, and instead of trying to train him up to rehome, which would've been very difficult as I would never have been able to trust that he wouldn't revert to his biting behavior, I decided I had to keep him and train him myself.

I spent many long hours teaching him to heel on the lead, giving him treats if he was able to walk the length of the yard without attempting to eat one of the animal residents. Eventually, with lots of patience on my part, and hard work on his, Harry calmed down, though he never lost that spark of naughtiness. It was Ben's arrival later that really softened Harry. Ben, a black Lab, had originally been a rescue dog, before belonging to one of our long-serving volunteers, Maggie. She had worked with us for eighteen years before she passed away, and I took Ben in in gratitude for Maggie's service.

At first I worried that Ben would pine for his mistress, but he settled down much quicker than I had expected, although for the first two nights he paced about, sniffing everywhere for his departed owner. Over time, his goofy grin, gentle ways, and sweet nature rubbed off on Harry, who stopped being mischievous and began to copy Ben. Previously Harry had only let the people he liked touch him or go near him. He'd always been very particular and could be unpredictable when meeting new people. After Ben's arrival, that all changed. Harry became a real sweetie and, following Ben's lead, he let people stroke him and rub his tummy, and even started bringing visitors little presents of a piece of discarded paper or a single shoe. It was adorable watching the two dogs teach each other the right way to behave.

Would the same happen with Gabby and Harry?

Every time Harry wanted to go outside, he looked back at Gabby, indicating she was to follow him, and Gabby would obediently get up and head after him. It was only when Harry disappeared out through the door that his pupil would stop, sniff the door, then back off, slinking back to her place next to my armchair, where coincidentally she'd just deposited her latest "gift" for me in the form of a poo.

"Oh Gabby, never mind, you didn't mean to do it I, know, but we must get you house-trained soon—I'm getting fed up of having to put down newspaper everywhere," I said kindly as I bent down to pick her up. She snuggled into my arms, her warm dog smell making me smile.

Taking in a rescue dog, or any animal, is an act of faith. It is an instinctive, from-the-heart decision that overrides any shred of practical or rational reasoning. Abandoned, mistreated, neglected, or simply unwanted dogs have a past that as the new owner we are unlikely to ever understand or know about. It is only over time that the traits of each animal, and the sum of their experiences in their former lives, come to the surface.

With Harry, it had been obvious to me that he had been mistreated and been left to run amok as he was willful and naughty, almost to the point of being untrainable. With Ben it was different. He'd been adored and treated well. Maggie had always given him the proper boundaries and gentleness that animals need to function normally.

With Gabby, it was obvious from the start how small her world had been. She'd stayed indoors her entire life. She'd never traveled in a car and found the experience terrifying, and she had never been house-trained. There were also other things that had emerged over those two weeks since she arrived. Gabby seemed to have no, or very subdued, hunter skills or desires. She didn't seem to want to chase or play with the other animals prowling around the site: the new peacock who displayed himself (though he'd lost his feathers for the summer) outside my window every morning, the cacophony of ducks, geese, chickens, roosters, and assorted birds that fluttered, strutted, called, and clucked in the yard outside. None of them seemed to inspire her to be curious about them; instead they remained a source of fear to her.

Gabby was happy with other dogs, which was a blessing. She'd grown up with the other three dogs owned by the elderly couple and so was at ease with canine companions. She was untrained generally and didn't seem to know what to do with commands such as "sit," "lie down," and "outside." However, she had the most wonderful gift of being able to make people smile. I'd noticed that she became the center of attention whenever the volunteers came in for coffee. She would be fussed over, tickled, stroked, and adored. Luckily, it had only taken Gabby ten days or so to realize that she liked being stroked. At first, I worried that she'd be overwhelmed by the attention, but strangely, it didn't appear to make her worse in that regard; instead she responded well to the fuss, though she still never made a sound.

Gabby just seemed to have that effect on people—they wanted to make a fuss over her. She was a very gentle dog, and I could see that more of her personality would come out over time, once she'd got past her nerves and the newness of her surroundings. There was no doubt, despite her issues, that Gabby and I had melded together in a way that went beyond mere words. Sometimes, a human and a dog find each other and fit together like two jigsaw pieces, and that's what it felt like with Gabby. She slept by my side every night, curled up against my body, my arm over her, almost as one person. Every day she stayed by my side, except when she was following Harry, and there was a definite synergy among the three of us. I'd never needed Harry more than at this moment. He was the key to Gabby becoming herself, and so I sat back and watched as he carried on guiding her, prompting her with a nudge or a sniff to walk in his paw steps, to be taught the things that every dog had in them from the moment they were born.

The morning of the Open Day arrived. It was a beautiful sunny morning, and there was a palpable sense of excitement at the sanctuary.

I had arisen at the crack of dawn, calling stallholders, finishing off the raffle tickets, and helping the others carry out straw bales and signposts to the fields at the site of the sanctuary.

Diane led the way as we walked down to the field, both of us carrying boxes.

"How's Gabby doing? Still not doing her business outside?" she asked, more to make conversation than anything as she already knew the ins and outs of my household.

"Well, she'll get there in her own time," I replied. "She's improving daily. Two weeks ago I'd never have thought she would be okay sitting with us in the living room or coping with all the volunteers coming inside for coffee. So all in all she's doing well. And how's my father lately?" I grinned.

The running joke was that the annex, which I'd built onto the house for my father's last years, was now haunted by him. Di had lived in the small space for many years now, and since his death we'd heard his voice many times, as distinct as anything. We'd hear "You there?" which was always what he said whenever anyone came into the house. When he was alive he'd call from the annex, checking we weren't burglars. Di also said how he enjoyed playing tricks on her.

"Ha yes, he's still there making mischief," she laughed. "Last night, in fact, I was hunting for my can opener, and I found it in my sock drawer!" I burst out laughing.

"He always did have a sense of humor, my dad. How did you ever think to look for it there?" I replied, putting the box down next to a booth selling things from our charity shop.

"I didn't! I found it later when I was getting ready for bed and looking for a pair of socks to wear. It isn't the first time he's hidden my cutlery or kitchen utensils. He went through a phase of stealing my knives and forks and placing them on my bookshelf!"

I thought for a moment about my father. I chuckled to myself as I remembered how he'd once brought home a monkey. It was after him and Mum had separated and he'd come to live with me in my ground-floor apartment in Eastbourne.

The fact that I lived in an apartment didn't bother him. He just walked in with this funny brown creature on his arm, saying he'd felt sorry for it. Apparently it looked really miserable in the pet shop window—he had to go in and buy it. I probably would've done the same.

Dad set about building a cage that took up half the small living room, made out of chicken wire and wood for support. Inside it were branches and plants, and it was where the cheeky little devil used to spend the night.

At first I was rather reluctant to have the monkey, which we called Bimbo, living with us, but after a while it became "normal." I even used to bathe it in a bucket of soapy water outside in the summer.

They were happy days. Dad's lovely, gentle, kindly face hovered in front of mine—his warm smile, his spectacles and graying hair—before I blinked and he vanished. I loved my father dearly, and still missed him, though I still felt his presence often. I'd nursed him at the end, bringing in his supper on a tray each evening and chatting at his bedside about all the goings-on of the day. As Dad was as besotted with animals as I was, he hung on every word, only interjecting to ask questions about specific animals, like: "What's happening to the

English bull terrier who needs a home? And the whippet, does anyone want him? What about the pig you need to go and get? Is he in yet? Where did you put him? He should go at the side, further up from the goats . . ."

I'd smile and patiently recount all the events of the day until he was too tired for me to continue. I would tuck him into bed, whisper "good night," and watch as he drifted into sleep. Losing him was very hard. Thank goodness I'd had the love and support of all the people—and animals—around me.

I stood for a moment, watching the hustle and bustle of people as they set things up. There was a bingo game and a raffle booth bursting with prizes donated by supporters. There were toy booths and art booths, crafts, and home baking. On the dot of 12 P.M. when the event opened, we would be inundated by people, all eager to help the sanctuary care for its animals. I felt a lump in my throat. People gave so much when it came to looking after the creatures we saved here.

I saw Diane looking animated and happy as she chatted to some locals who came every year. I watched as Brenda helped an elderly couple fill out one of the animal sponsorship forms. She was such a professional. I didn't know what I'd do without her. Dan appeared from the yard carrying a piled-up concertina of plastic chairs for the visitors who were streaming in through the gates. Here and there, people busied themselves, selling raffle tickets, showing visitors the cattery and its residents, serving teas and scones in the small on-site café we were hoping to expand next year. There was a pleasant throng of activity, the sound of people laughing, joking, and generally enjoying themselves.

By 5 P.M. I was shattered, but I always stayed until the last visitor had left and the last coins and pound notes had been counted. Fran was beaming when he walked over to me about an hour after we'd finally shut the gates, all of us heaving a sigh of relief and nursing the feeling we'd all done a great job that day.

"We're at least a thousand pounds up on last year," he said, offering me the notebook with his line of figures marching to the end of the page.

"How much do you reckon?" I asked, shading my eyes from the sun that was still warm.

"Around eight thousand, give or take a few quid," he replied, and I smiled back at him. That would keep us going for some time. It had indeed been a good day.

Chapter 7

LEARNING HOW TO PLAY

For me, the saddest thing about Gabby, compared to all the other hundreds of abandoned dogs I'd fostered at the sanctuary, was the fact that she didn't know how to play.

Play is an essential part of a dog's experience of the world; in fact, most of the time it isn't really play at all, it's a throwback to the more primal animal urges to stalk prey, pounce on the creatures they hunt, and fight for territory or food. Watching dogs play, and their obvious delight in rolling around on the floor, their playful snarls and yelps as they get down to the bare basics of their wolf nature, is always a delight to me. It's the way dogs learn and express their true spirits.

That Gabby still seemed confused at the array of stuffed animals and cuddly toys that lay in various states of dishevelment on the living room floor broke my heart. It showed me how little exposure she'd had to pure animalistic joy, and I was determined to help her embrace the fun of being a dog. I decided to try playing with the toy fox again.

"Now then Gabby, stop looking at me like I've gone mad. I'm going to show you how to pretend to eat this furry fox, just like Harry and Ben."

I was standing in front of Gabby, who was sitting opposite me on the hearth rug, looking at me for all the world like she was thinking: "What are you doing now, Mum?" Her head was cocked to one side, and her inquisitive gaze held mine.

"Okay, here I go, now grab the toy, go on, grab it and bite it and throw it on the floor. Pretend this is a real fox, not a stuffed one, and let rip on it . . ."

I jumped up and down in front of her, waving the fox at nose height and making growling noises. I gnashed my teeth, shook the fox, and pretended to pounce upon it, ending up on all fours on the rug alongside the bemused dog. As before, Gabby just sat and stared, her gorgeous brown eyes peering into mine, clearly utterly bewildered. I burst out laughing.

I was a little out of breath, and I took a moment to gather myself. "You won't see me doing that too often, Gabby, so you might as well make the most of it. This is how dogs like you have fun. You've seen Harry and Ben fight over this fox, now why don't you try and get it off me, come on, give it a go . . ."

I waved the toy yet again in front of her.

Gabby made a small whining sound and lay down, putting her head onto her paws, her eyes never leaving my face.

"I'm going to have to try a bit harder, aren't I? But I won't give up, oh no, that's not something I ever do!" I smiled at my hound, flopping down on the rug next to her and stroking her shining fur.

I was right on that. Since buying the land, I'd built up the sanctuary bit by bit, by the skin of my teeth with little or no money to speak of. This steely focus had stood me well over time. Alongside my partner at the time, Les, I had built my own house on the land. I'd grouted tiles, whitewashed walls, and helped lay brick after brick. I didn't stand around watching others do the work. I was a worker and I always got stuck in.

Les was a devilishly handsome man, but he had one big flaw. He wouldn't stand up for himself. When Rother District Council planners got wind of the small bungalow we'd built using our own hands, they came and visited, shook their heads, and immediately ordered it to be knocked down as we'd built without planning consent. Naively, I'd left all the paperwork to Les, assuming that he would sort out that kind of thing. I was too focused on my animals, as by then I had horses, ponies, a cow, sheep, dogs, cats and various rabbits, guinea pigs, and birds. I had no spare time, and absolutely no inclination, to fill out forms.

The day the bulldozer arrived to knock our home down— the house that I had lovingly decorated, the living room I had painted, the bathroom I had tiled myself—I packed up my dogs (Pip, a spaniel; Hercules, a Saint Bernard; Blackie, a Tibetan terrier; Caddy, a Labrador; Tramp, another Labrador cross; and Zede, a German shepherd, into Les's car and drove away, unable to look back at the destruction. As I pulled out onto the lane I heard the "whump" of the first hammer blow, yet I didn't cry. My eyes remained dry. It was just a house, just bricks and mortar, and I knew I'd been through worse. As a seven-year-old child I'd returned from being evacuated to find our home a pile of smoking rubble, courtesy of the Luftwaffe.

All I had was contained in the small suitcase I held in my hand, all except a pink fluffy rabbit toy that one of the firefighters fetched for me from inside the ruins. So I knew what it was to be homeless, to feel the utter blank horror of knowing there was no home to sleep in that night. Knocking down that house brought it all back, along with the resilience and determination not to be affected by it. A house was just a house, a home could be made anywhere, or that's what I'd learned.

After that, we moved back into the two trailers that I'd originally placed on the site, me and Les in one, and my dad in the other. Mine leaked every time it rained, and I had to place saucepans under the drips, day and night. Fed up with knocking over buckets, I eventually drilled holes in the floor of the RV to let out the excess water. It was perishingly cold in the winter and ferociously hot in the summer, yet I survived living like that for the next twenty years until I could afford to rebuild.

There were good times, like the evenings Les and I spent giggling at the sheep that had decided it was our dog, and so spent each evening trying to curl her large frame into the armchair. One day we had a visitor, who sat in the living room, sipping his tea, chatting away to us. When he got up to leave, he said: "May I ask you a question? Is there a sheep sitting in the corner armchair watching the television?"

Les and I shrieked with laughter. The poor man thought he was going mad. We were all too happy to tell him he wasn't! That particular sheep had been hand-reared by a doting farmer who had dogs, and so thought it was a canine, too. It was so used to being inside that when it wanted to do a wee, it would stand with its legs apart, and Les or I would have to leap for the bucket we called the "yellow peril" and dive over to catch the wee before it hit the floor. Funny times, but it was tough.

I refused to give up on the sanctuary then, even when it seemed impossible to survive another month both financially and because of the strained living conditions, yet I kept going.

I was now determined to use that same fierce strength to keep my focus on Gabby. I couldn't bear seeing her so timid, jumping at each strange new noise and not daring to step outside, the most natural thing in the world for a dog to do. I wouldn't give up on her, as I kept telling her.

Gabby had been with me for a month now, and had taken a few baby steps forward. She had learned not to venture into my bedroom to poo or wee, which was naturally a blessing. Also, she still hadn't gone beyond sniffing the dog door, but whenever Harry went out she would now sit by the open French doors that looked onto my sunroom and watch him go past.

"She's building up to going outside, I'm sure of it," I said to Di one afternoon at the end of August.

We were walking back from the cattery toward the bungalow as the late afternoon light danced through the branches of trees close to the house. I sighed and stopped for a moment, breathing in the warm summer smells. They were good, honest countryside scents, the kind that you discover as a child and dream of as an adult. Scanning the landscape, I saw the sanctuary as if through another's eyes, and sometimes I simply couldn't believe how big the place had grown and how many animals were being loved and protected here.

The sanctuary is made up of twelve acres, of which the bungalow sat at the heart and was opposite the cattery, which was being extended with a cat hospital and new pens for the adoptable cats. The cattery was sealed off with wire fencing, but we had feral cats who slept there overnight and disappeared each morning. To the left of the bungalow was the steel gate leading to the farm animals' enclosures.

Beyond the gates were fields for horses and ponies, and the pens for the goats with their funny little wooden "houses" banked up with straw. In the winter you could only see their horns curling over the hay. There were sheep held there, too, and there was a muddy path that led down to the pigs. The pigs had large areas, fenced off with sturdy posts and bigger sheds.

Behind all this were the outer rims of the land, the places we kept wild horses and untamable goats. The path that went past the pigs wound down to the back of the land, which my bungalow looked out upon. Here there was the aviary for the sick and injured birds, and the telegraph poles that became the resting place for the hundreds of birds that swooped down for their breakfast each morning. If you kept walking in a circle, you'd then come to the kennels, the workrooms, and the fields for the ponies. A couple of trailers squatted behind the workspace, which housed the machinery, the wood saws and all the equipment we needed on a daily basis to build fencing, signs, enclosures and everything else.

The dogs were barking in their kennels that lay by the large gated entrance to the sanctuary, as they were being given their dinner by a volunteer, the sound carrying across the site. By the time my gaze reached the kennels, Di had noticed I'd stopped and so she halted and smiled with me.

"It's quite a sight," she said.

I nodded. I could never have imagined that all this would be created by my simple desire to care for animals.

"Let's go in," I said, suddenly embarrassed by my intro-spection. "I have a dog that needs to learn how to play . . ." Back inside, I was greeted by Harry and Ben in their usual boisterous, joyful way as Gabby shrunk behind them. Her eyes found mine, though, and I knew she was as pleased to see me as the others but just didn't know how to express it yet.

"Listen to me, girl," I chatted brightly as I scooped her up into my arms, "we're going to try and have a little play again. You'll like that, I promise."

Gabby sniffed at me, licking my chin as her tail wagged against my hip.

"Good girl, that's right, give me a good once-over. Do I smell of the cats, my darling?" I crooned. I really had fallen head over heels for this one.

I put Gabby down on the rug and went to fetch an array of toys; a blue squeaky plastic bone, a teddy bear that had seen better days, and a stick from the garden.

"Now then, Gabby, which one would you like to try?" I said, placing all three objects in front of her.

Gabby sat staring at me blankly. There was no recognition in her eyes.

"The only way to teach you how to play is to keep showing

you," I smiled, "and I won't stop making a fool of myself until you get it. Look, here comes Ben, he's the best one to help us . . . Come on, Ben, come on boy, yes, let's play with this, grrrrr." I got onto my knees and waved the teddy bear in front of him. He didn't hesitate for a moment.

Ben sprang into life. His body tensed, he moved closer to the floor, his belly almost touching the rug as he snarled and generally reacted in a menacing way. Then he pounced, attacking the teddy bear with gleeful abandon, and at that point Harry joined in.

The pale golden-haired spaniel and the black Lab tussled and tumbled on the floor, rolling over and over as they fought each other for the teddy bear.

"Here's the squeaky bone! Who wants the bone?" I laughed, as Harry turned to me, dropping hold of the teddy bear's ear and leaping for the bone. I threw it in a corner of the room, and he skidded over to it, grabbing it between his teeth and shaking it, grappling with it using his head and mouth with much joyful growling.

My gaze darted to Gabby. She was watching the two dogs intently. I could see recognition of their games on her face, a kind of understanding, but she still didn't move. It was very frustrating.

"Come on, Gabby, let's see if you can chase this stick," I said as I threw it to the other corner of the room, which wasn't far, but enough to show the dog what I was encouraging her to do.

Still nothing. Gabby was sitting, staring at the stick and

then back at me as if to say, "What do you mean—I have to fetch the stick?!"

I couldn't help but laugh. Then I spotted a ball underneath the sofa and so I bent over and retrieved it. Kneeling down directly in front of Gabby, I used my softest voice to say, "Here, darling, let's play together, see what that naughty Ben does with the squeaky ball . . ." and Ben, on seeing the new toy, leapt up and rolled himself into a playful fury of fur and movement, fooling around with the ball. His eyes rolled in his head, his tongue lolled out of his mouth—he really was quite a sight.

Gabby looked confused. She stood up and stepped back but stayed watching until eventually Ben lost interest and wandered off, leaving the toy abandoned on the rug.

Instinct told me to stay quiet, and to stay still. Gabby looked at me as if to say "What now?" and I just gave her a smile.

Then, as if by magic, Gabby put one paw out and touched the ball, instantly recoiling as if it was a step too far.

That's it, girl, try again . . . I thought to myself, not daring to make a sound in case I distracted her attention.

When nothing happened, she reached out and pawed it again, this time making it roll just a little. Then, when the sky didn't fall in, and she felt her confidence returning, she pushed it again.

"That's it, Gabby, that's it . . . you're starting to play!" I couldn't help it now. I was so thrilled that she'd interacted with the toy that my words burst out of me. I clapped my hands with joy.

"Now why don't we see what this teddy bear feels like?
See how fluffy he is . . ." I kept speaking now, willing the dog
to keep exploring the toys, to keep reconnecting with her primal past. She didn't go for the other toys straight away, but
I knew now that we had made a breakthrough. This small
touch of a toy was a real glimmer of hope that I was getting
through to this dear little dog.

Chapter 8

Steps Forward

Marching out toward the feline immunodeficiency virus (FIV) area, where we house cats with the feline equivalent of the AIDS virus, I heard the slam of the dog door behind me as Ben dashed out to join me.

"We're just going to check in with Diane as there are a few cats that need attending to. You won't be able to follow me in there, Ben, my dear," I chuckled.

I looked down at the soppy dog with his dark eyes and scruffy black fur, bending to tickle him on the nose before continuing on my way.

"Di, how are things?" I called as I arrived. It was just a short walk of a few meters to the FIV area, which was cordoned off with wire that stretched around the structure and over the roof to prevent any of the cats escaping and potentially infecting others with the disease that destroys a cat's immunity to viruses and generally compromises its immune system.

I opened the door, making sure Ben didn't wind in around

my legs, and that in the process I didn't let any of the cats run out, either. Ben stood outside the cage with big mournful eyes, his tongue hanging out.

"Sorry, boy, I won't be a moment." I scrabbled around in my pocket to find a chew I'd remembered to bring for him and threw it back out. *That should keep him amused for a few moments at least*, I thought.

I didn't have to worry about catching anything inside the area. Humans aren't susceptible to FIV, and cats usually catch it through fighting with an infected cat and being bitten or drawing blood. Some experts think it is also passed through sex, like the human version, but I'd heard that was uncertain, and possibly more the result of the male cat biting the female's neck to keep her in place while mating with her. Saying that, I encouraged my staff and volunteers to use the squirters of hand sanitizer that were dotted about the site. This was as much to do with not passing any illnesses to the animals as to protect us against germs.

Cats with the condition can usually have a relatively normal life span if they find somewhere like the Animal Sanctuary, where they can live out the rest of their days in comfort and with proper care and regular medical checkups. As far as I was aware, at the time we were the only shelter in the UK that took in FIV-positive cats, though there were places in Europe.

"Morning, Barby, well, I've got Lily who needs to be de-matted at the vets because she's too fluffy. Poppy is the new Romanian one who came in overnight, so she needs to be checked over, and Kipling who is still having problems with his bladder," said Di. Kipling had come to us after being run over. It was only during the treatment of his crushed bowels and kidneys that FIV was diagnosed.

Di was busy putting down bowls of water, stopping to stroke the cats as they mewed for their breakfast and wound their tails around her. Di was besotted with cats. She had several of her own that lived with her in her annex, including Rhianna, an ex–street cat who had bitten ears and white fur with black patches.

"Okay dear, will you call the vet and sort those out? I'd better go back and write that lot down in the book before I forget."

My meticulous note-taking was as much to keep an eye on each animal's progress as to record all the possible expenditure. My vets' bills ran into thousands every month, but what else could I do? There was no way I'd let an animal suffer, even if we had to economize elsewhere.

"Gabby still not coming outside?" Di asked.

"No, she still hasn't made it. There have been a few times I thought, yes, perhaps she'll do it today. These days she puts her nose almost through the gap in the wall, but at the last minute she panics and runs off. She's a darling, and such an anxious little thing that I can't get upset with her. She'll do it in her own time. . . ."

"Are you sure of that?" Di interjected.

I shook my head. "I wish I was. I hate seeing her inside all day. She almost squashes her nose on the glass doors watching Harry and Ben go outside so I'm thinking she must *want* to go, it's just that she's scared. What she doesn't realize is

that I'd fight off any intruders or scary things to protect her,"
I said fiercely, only half joking.

I've always had a temper. I inherited it from my mother.
If people think I'm feisty, then they should've met her. As
children, my brother Peter and I called her "grizzly bear,"
and she certainly lived up to her name. She would fight off
anyone who threatened us, but sadly she also behaved like
that in the home, mostly venting her furies on me; I was a
cross, screwed-up-face kind of child, so I didn't blame her
for that. I certainly made life difficult for her with my grumps
and my defiance. I would pretty much refuse anything she
offered me to eat or wear, and in those days there was little
choice. We battled throughout my childhood, both of us with
strong personalities, until she and Dad split up when I was
in my twenties. From that moment I rarely saw her. Our lives
separated, and I found to my shame that I didn't miss her.
She rarely contacted me, either, and, sadly, we became es-
tranged. When she died, many years ago now, I went to her
funeral, but that enmity and the historic lack of warmth in
our relationship was so strong, so present, that I felt like a
fraud at the service, and couldn't wait to get away afterward.

I marked her passing in my own way later that day by taking a long walk with Pip, my spaniel, and Zede, my German
shepherd. I walked and walked over my fields, soaking up the
landscape, the leaves turning brown for autumn, the sharp
distinctive scent of woodsmoke in the air. I remembered her
in my own way, and mostly I felt grief for what should have
been, rather than what had been. I'd probably yearned as a
child for the natural love and comfort only a mother can bring,

yet I never received it. I was well cared for practically, I couldn't ever fault her for that. I always had clean clothes, school uniform and shoes, and there was always something to eat and a place to sleep, but I always knew there was little love lost between us, a knowledge that has confused me and saddened me throughout my whole life.

I'd recalled how one evening, when I was twelve years old, she'd told me to take some pennies from her purse and run to the butcher to buy four meat pies for supper. I ran off, reached the shop, and walked in, spotting four tasty-looking pies on the counter.

The butcher, a kindly family man with thinning hair, a big gut, and a warm smile, said to me in a booming voice, "Can I help you, little madam?"

"No, I don't need any help. I want those." I pointed at the pies with their golden pastry and pouted, sticking my chin up. I didn't need any help, and I never asked it of anyone. I have always been a self-reliant sort of person.

"Okay dear. I'll wrap them up for you. You say hello to your mother, d'you hear me, young lady?"

I nodded and grabbed the parcel, feeling the warm food inside, leaving Mother's coins on the counter.

Mum nodded when I returned, saying only, "Sit down. Your supper is ready once these pies are on your plates."

Peter was already sitting at the table. Gorgeous, happy-go-lucky, golden-haired Peter. I grinned at him, and he said, "You in trouble again, Barby?" It was our standing joke, because somehow I was always in trouble with our mother, whatever I did, or didn't do. I'd always done *something* wrong.

"Not this time," I said, poking my tongue out at him and making him giggle.

Mum brought the plates to the table. We each had two potatoes, some green beans from Dad's allotment, and gravy, which I poured liberally over the pie. Imagine our horror when we sliced into it. The pies were apple pies, not meat ones. My willfulness had been rewarded with the wrong supper. Mother was furious. Peter started giggling and so I kicked him under the table, my disappointment was so acute. Mother sent me to my room without any dinner, both for kicking Peter and for bringing back the wrong pies. I wasn't cross about that. I knew even at that young age that I thoroughly deserved my punishment.

I'm still the same person today.

A few years ago, a new set of neighbors bought the house next door to the sanctuary. Only days after they'd arrived, council officers arrived at my gate demanding to know why the animals made such a noise. The neighbors had complained about the dogs barking, the roosters crowing, and the sheep baaing—after buying a house next door to an animal shelter! It beggared belief.

I was so furious that they'd complained—and had got me into trouble with the council noise abatement services—that I marched down my lane with a shovel intending to whack their gate in order to make even more noise. I was boiling with anger.

Luckily Dan saw me heading out and ran after me, stopping me in my tracks before I could vent my fury. My trusty farm manager made me stop, talked me down from my righteous rage, and led me back into the sanctuary with no harm done or further problems caused. When I'm angry, it's always with people, never with animals. Animals are pure instinct. They don't try to manipulate or harm anyone or anything outside of their need to eat, sleep, and procreate. They act out of need rather than spite, and perhaps this is another reason I've always found animals easier to love than humans.

I was brought out of my daydream by the phone ringing.

"Yes, . . ." I said as I picked it up, looking around the front room for Gabby. No doubt it would be somebody in need of the shelter for their pet.

"Hello, my darling," I smiled as Gabby walked in to find me, coming straight to me and settling down at my feet.

"No, sorry dear, not you," I apologized to the caller.

"How can I help you?"

"We've got a collie dog we can't keep any longer. We're getting too old to exercise him and he needs at least three big walks a day. We're so sorry, but we're going to have to rehome him." It was a woman's voice, clearly elderly, on the other end.

"Okay dear. You're in luck; I think we have a space in the kennels. I'll get Dan or Fran to call you once they've checked. Can you wait until later today?"

The woman said yes, and I was relieved. Some people only contacted us when they were at breaking point with their pet, and the temptation was always to dump the animal if they couldn't wait any longer to bring it to us.

I said good-bye and called over the walkie-talkie system to Dan, giving him their number. Then I looked down at my pooch. Gabby was gazing up at me so sweetly. I pulled her up onto my lap and felt that happiness that only stroking a beloved hound can bring.

Then the walkie-talkie buzzed for me. It was Dan's voice.

"I need you to come out here, as we need to talk about the dogs. There's a pit bull that's due to be rehomed but I'm not sure when and who's having him . . ."

"Okay Dan, I'm on my way," I said a little wearily. I was up and down all day, in and out of the bungalow, never seeming to get as much work done as I'd like.

"You be a good girl, Gabby, and stay in here. Now you've relaxed a little you can have a go playing with the ball, and you can have a chew on the pretend bone as well. I won't be long, lovely one . . ."

Gabby hated me going out. She didn't make a huge fuss, but the look in her eyes was one of utter abandonment as she implored me to stay. This time I grabbed my padded vest to throw on. Gabby had been with us for just over three months now, and outside the leaves were turning brown and the sky was overcast. To my disappointment, Gabby still hadn't learned to do her business in the litter tray I had provided, and was still having accidents, though mostly in the kitchen, the floor of which was still permanently covered in newspaper. Autumn had come, and I'd felt chilly earlier while out with the cats. It was time to wrap up warm again after the mellow days of summer.

Striding out of the front door after pulling my wellies back on, I heard the click of the dog door as Harry came through it. It was his turn to follow me.

Then I heard the strangest sound. The door clicked again. I knew Ben was sleeping on my bed, so it couldn't be him, I thought as I turned round, puzzled.

"It can't be . . ." I started to say, but there she was. Gabby was standing outside of the doorway, looking as starstruck as if she had arrived on the moon. She looked stunned, then her doggie instincts kicked in, and my honey-colored mutt tentatively put her nose to the ground and started sniffing it for new smells. Harry trotted back to her, ever her protector, and she looked up at him, her face still registering the shock of the outdoors, the space, the light, even though it was gray, and the breeze that caught the tumbled-down leaves and shifted them slightly at her feet.

That seemed to wake her from her dreaming. She looked over at me again, as if to say, "Mummy, I've done it!"

"Gabby! You clever dog!" I laughed, feeling an extraordinary sense of achievement on her behalf. My heart was in my mouth as I looked at her. I didn't say a word. I didn't want to break the spell, the magic of her finally being outside. She looked momentarily confused again, then she surveyed the scene, the acres of space, the chickens and hens clucking nearby, the geese shaking their tail feathers, the birds flitting between branches. It must have been overwhelming, yet her tail started to wag.

At that moment, my eyes welled up with tears.

Silly Barby, stop that immediately, I admonished myself.

"Come on, girl, come on, Harry, there's work to do," I said gruffly, the words catching in my throat as I turned to walk onward. I knew it was probably too much to expect of her to follow me on her first outing, but I also didn't want to make a fuss in case that stopped her.

As I suspected, I looked back just as the door clicked shut again, this time with Gabby behind it. She had turned tail and with a clack of the door she had retreated out of the cold and back into the safety of her known world. Harry was still at my heels as we kept going, the dogs in the kennels barking to announce our arrival. It was literally a small step for Gabby but to me, it felt like a huge leap forward.

Chapter 9

SMALL STEPS

Knock knock!

Harry leapt up off the rug, Ben close behind him, both barking as they dashed to the doorway.

"Shush now, you two, come on, get out of my way, silly dogs, and let me see who it is. It's probably just the mailman," I laughed.

I was right. The mailman, a young-looking man, was standing outside. I shooed the dogs away as he handed me a pile of envelopes.

"Might be a few bills in there, I'm afraid," he joked, but he was right.

Leafing through them I headed back to the living room, counting the number of brown envelopes that included our gas and electricity bills, a statement from the vet, and a few other handwritten letters, mostly letters of thanks or small donations sent in by supporters. Every day I marveled at how generous people were, and how even the least affluent managed to send in a few pounds every year to help our work.

Frowning at the bills, I looked down. Two eager faces looked up at me—the third, Gabby's, was missing.

"One day, Gabby," I called out, "you'll copy Harry and Ben and come running to bite off the mailman's head, barking loudly."

At least I hoped she would. Gabby's silence still bothered me. A dog who couldn't bark—who had ever heard of such a thing?

We knew there was no medical reason for it—she'd been thoroughly checked over by a vet at home within a day or two of her arriving.

"There's nothing wrong with her throat," the vet, Stephen, had said. "There are no lesions, no swelling, nothing obstructing it. Judging by her temperament, I'd say she was shocked into silence and that only time will tell if she'll ever bark. Other than the fact she's very anxious, she's in surprisingly good shape. She's obviously been fed well and looked after. Her coat is glossy, there are no scars or any other signs of mistreatment or neglect, so I'd say it was down to you now, Barby." Stephen looked at me and I shrugged. Well, I knew that already!

Since then, Gabby had tried to make sounds, or at least that was how I interpreted the noises coming from her. Over the months since her arrival, she had learned to make whinnying noises, stretching her mouth as if a noise was about to come out. She was making such a noise now as she appeared from my bedroom, pawing my leg in the hope of being picked up. I bent over and pulled her up into my arms. I could never resist a cuddle with her.

"Never mind, girl, we can wait for that bark, we know it's in there somewhere," I smiled, and Harry barked as if in agreement.

At that moment I had a brainstorm. I gripped Gabby round her tummy and held her on my left hip like a mum with her toddler, while I reached for the phone. After three rings my old friend Ivy picked up.

"Hello, dear, do you fancy a visit? I haven't seen you in ages."

"Hello, Barby, yes, that would be wonderful. Will you be bringing Gabby with you?" she asked. Ivy had taken in Kenny and Jessy, Gabby's half-siblings, and we had been speaking regularly as I tried to piece together Gabby's backstory in relation to how Kenny and Jessy behaved.

"Yes, now that she's becoming more comfortable with being outside, I feel sure that a trip in the car won't leave her feeling as shell-shocked this time.

"I do have an ulterior motive for coming, it's not just to see you my dear . . ." I added, teasing my friend a little, but with deadly intent.

"What's that, Barby?" Ivy asked.

"Well, Gabby is coming on well, she's eating, sleeping next to me, playing with toys, but she's still not barking, and I'm getting worried about her. She's been with me for three months and still nothing. I'm hoping that seeing her siblings will jog her memory, assuming she barked in her previous life, or will spur her into making some noise of her own. It's the only thing I can think of to do . . ."

Ivy was only too happy to help, and we made arrangements to see each other in a few days' time.

There is always an adjustment period when a foster dog settles into a new home, and Gabby was clearly no exception. I knew that during those first few weeks, or even months, she would have been stressed, and unsure about how long her new place would last. It always takes time for an animal to understand that they have found their forever home.

Gabby had been with us for four months, and ever since that first tentative step outside, I'd spent lots of time taking her outside to start the process of familiarizing her with the surrounding environment. At first she wouldn't go farther than a few steps into the yard, and she jumped at every squawk or grunt. I plied her with doggie treats as I coaxed her into going a little farther each day. Even a small breeze or an insect could catch her off guard, and, when that happened, she'd turn tail and head back indoors. I didn't mind though. I could see that each day she was becoming a little braver, a little more sure of herself, although when the day of our trip to Ivy's came around I was still worried about how she would react as it involved being put back in a car again.

On the morning of the visit, I made sure that my car was filled with her blankets and bed so that she would hopefully feel comforted on the short drive into Bexhill. I chatted away to her as I drove, telling her how brave she was for coming and how wonderful it would be to see her "siblings" again.

Gabby stayed completely silent, except for that half-yawn, half-grimace thing she did with her mouth, which was a sign of stress. At one point I almost turned back. It is hard to push boundaries, and I wondered if I was doing too much, too fast, for her. Yawning was her way of releasing tension as we traveled, and the most I heard from her was a slight whine as she stretched her jaws. I decided to keep going, talking soothingly as we went. If at any moment she had become very panicked, rather than just anxious, I would have turned back, but she was coping, just, so I kept going.

Upon arrival, I carried her out of the car. I didn't want her to register the new feeling of gravel underfoot, and I wasn't sure how she'd react to walking on grass, either, as she'd never done it before. In the weeks I'd been spending time with Gabby outdoors, the farthest we'd reached were the pathways around the sanctuary, with Gabby keeping to the paved areas. I hadn't wanted to push her more than she was ready for, so I had contented myself with these small excursions, until now. It made me feel so sad. A dog who hadn't played in the grass— now that was inconceivable to me.

We went in through the side gate, and I saw Ivy sitting in the garden watching Kenny and Jessy play on the lawn. They were chasing each other and rolling over and over in unfeigned delight at the open space.

"Hello, it's Barby," I called as I walked over.

"Hello dear, oh is that Gabby? She is a lovely little thing, isn't she," Ivy smiled.

I sat down on one of the garden chairs, keeping Gabby close to me in my arms. She had started to tremble so I stroked her and whispered quietly to her to reassure her.

"Who's that then? Who are those two dogs, eh?" I said, making my voice as bright as possible as they bounded up to greet us.

Gabby looked at them and instantly there was recognition

on her face. The delight on Kenny and Jessy's faces was plain to see. They both sniffed Gabby, and she sat up, her tail wagging ever so slightly, and I gently placed her down on the grass.

"It's Kenny and Jessy. Why don't you have a play with them?" I said, not thinking for a minute that she would walk off. But Gabby looked up at me as if to say "Okay, Mummy," before cautiously trotting off with them.

I felt a lump in my throat. She was smelling the grass, peering round at the open space, and she hadn't backed off, she was even trying to explore it.

"This is a major breakthrough!" I said delightedly. "I don't know why I didn't think of this earlier. It's good to socialize Gabby. She has learned to get on with Harry and Ben, but it must be so good for her to see Kenny and Jessy because they're so familiar."

Ivy and I looked over at them. Kenny and Jessy were pretending to stalk each other, backing off then leaping with lots of friendly playful snarling. Gabby eyed them both with curiosity rather than fear. Her ears were up. She wasn't displaying any signs of nerves, just inquisitiveness. I could have clapped with sheer happiness.

"Come on, girl. Have a play, you know you want to . . ." I muttered, watching her like a hawk. She looked unsure but she wasn't trying to leave. That had to be a good sign, as was the fact that she had stepped onto the grass without any adverse reaction. It was another milestone reached.

"The big question is, Barby, is she house-trained yet?"

laughed Ivy, distracting me. She had a good sense of humor—
that's why we got on, though she did like to talk.

I'd known my friend for years, and she was an animal lover
through and through. She lived by herself and was devoted
to the dogs, that much was clear. I often called her to chat
about the events of the day and she was always interested in
hearing about the comings and goings at the sanctuary.

"Not yet, but she'll get there. I'm having to use all the volunteers' newspapers every day to put over the floor and that's
not going down well," I guffawed, feeling a sudden release of
the tight band of tension around my chest. Gabby was now
trotting round the garden, following the scents probably left
by foxes overnight, smelling the plants and flowers. She wasn't
yet joining in the other dogs' games, but she was looking happier and more confident with each moment that passed.

Ivy and I chatted about the sanctuary and the day-to-day
challenges we always faced. Time passed as we talked.

By now, Gabby was enjoying herself, running between each
dog as they tumbled and chased each other across the grass.
Ivy served tea and biscuits and we spent a pleasant afternoon
together as the dogs played, though Gabby still made no
sound, even when Kenny and Jessy barked playfully as part
of their fun.

"Well, you've got a pair of fantastic guard dogs," I said,
sipping my tea.

"They've been wonderful, really, Barby, I haven't had any
trouble from either of them. It took a couple of days for them
to settle in but really, there were no problems at all."

"Were they house-trained when they arrived?" I asked, wanting to know as much about Gabby's history, and that of her siblings, as I could.

"They were. They both went outside from day one. They were both well trained. It seems so peculiar that Gabby wasn't."

I nodded. It was a strange situation, and I really had to accept that I would never know why Gabby was like she was. All I could do was try to help her learn how to do the things that most dogs did without thinking.

"Perhaps the couple became too ill to train her. If I had to guess the reason, it would be that. My feel is that Kenny and Jessy arrived before Gabby did, and were properly socialized and house-trained, whereas when Gabby came along, the effort may have proved too much for them. They are both very poorly now and have gone into nursing homes, so it must've been a struggle having three dogs to care for." I sighed. "Fostering dogs is really about taking on an unknown quantity. You never know what lies in their past—and it's pointless guessing," I added.

Both Ivy and I looked over at the dogs. Gabby was sitting to the side of them, watching them roll over each other. Brown, curled leaves lay under the trees that surrounded the garden, and the wind was rather chilly despite it being a mild autumn afternoon. When Ivy shivered I stood up.

"We should be going, it's getting cold out here." I called to Gabby, and she ran over immediately. "Good girl, here's a treat. Oh go on then, one for you Kenny, and for you Jessy as well."

Later, once we were back at the site, I took Gabby out for

a walk. She had coped extremely well with the drive home, and I wanted to capitalize on the leaps and bounds she'd made today.

"Let's check on the animals together this evening, darling," I said as we walked off companionably. I didn't bother getting a lead as I knew that she would hover as close to me as she could get, if she came all the way round the site at all.

"Let's go and meet the other residents. I'm sure they'll want to meet you, my darling."

We walked down the higgledy-piggledy garden path, Gabby looking up at me every few feet as if to say "Is it all okay?" and so I kept reassuring her, and giving her the treats she liked. She suddenly stopped and started sniffing at the hedge. I thought perhaps there was a rabbit or mouse that had caught her attention, but she started walking round in circles before coming to a stop once more. Gingerly, she flattened her lower body against the grass. I held my breath. I knew what that stance meant. "Go on, girl," I muttered to myself. And sure enough, she did a wee by the hedgerow. Never had I ever been so happy to see an animal go to the toilet! I made sure I gave her lots of praise and another doggie treat to reinforce her good behavior.

When one of the horses, a wild-caught mare who had been left in a field after the farmer sold up and moved away, neighed rather too close to her, she almost lost her nerve, skittering back to hide behind my legs.

"It's okay, girl, it's just Pickle the horse, she is still getting used to us, too," I said, holding Gabby's black, gold, and white head gently between my hands. Gabby had frozen at the sound of the horse's whinnying, and I had to coax her away from the area with another treat and some soft words.

"Now let's go and see if Houdini has managed to escape his pen yet." We walked off together, further down to the back fields where the goat who was our resident escapologist was fenced in. He was still there. I leaned on the wooden gate and peered over at him. Houdini was a pale white-and-brown goat with curled horns and a fierce temperament.

"Stay well away from him. He doesn't like being restricted by a fence. He'd be out of the field and off given half the chance," I chuckled. Gabby looked up at me in her soulful way, as if she was listening to every word.

I mused for a moment on the difference between Houdini, who couldn't wait to be free, and the little dog beside me, who was having to be coaxed out at every turn, and the time and effort it had taken to get her this far. No two animals could have been more different.

"Come on, Gabby, time for supper and bed," I said, casting a last look at the goat, who eyed me from the corner of his vision, chewing on long strands of grass. I couldn't help but laugh at the absurdity of it all.

Chapter 10

Doing The Right Thing

Barking is natural to all breeds of dog as a form of communication. It can be an alert, telling the pack that danger approaches, or that the house is on fire or being raided by burglars. It can also be used by dogs as a way to demand food or attention, and can escalate into a toddler-style temper tantrum if they aren't given that tidbit or can't run after the cat that is within sight. Barking can be a sign of worry or stress, and often accompanies separation anxiety, with howling and panicky noises as well. Even boredom can be a source of barking; when dogs are left by themselves they often react by barking as they are pack animals and feel isolation keenly. When dogs play, they often bark as a sign of their enjoyment, and my dogs Harry and Ben were no exception, yapping and growling as they tumbled together. Gabby had been with me for six months and still hadn't made a proper sound. I had come to the conclusion that she would probably never bark, and the thought made me feel strangely sad. This was the last "dog" action she had yet to master, or relearn. I wondered if, by letting her come to each new hurdle in her own time, I'd inadvertently allowed her to settle without the key skill of barking.

Pondering this, I opened the door to the mailman I'd seen walking across the yard. It was a bitterly cold January morning and I took the proffered letters as quickly as I could without causing offense.

"Sorry, I don't want to let the heat out. Thank you," I said as I closed the door, shivering a little with the chill, and waving away Henrietta the football-mad chicken, who had flapped up onto the kitchen cabinets. At the age of sixty-eight (only a few short weeks away from my sixty-ninth birthday), I was starting to feel the cold in a way I never used to.

Flicking through the envelopes, I saw a large white one with an NHS stamp on the front. Puzzled, I opened it to find a letter from my doctor and scanned it quickly. I was being told to go for a routine mammogram.

"Well, I don't have time to be doing that now, do I Gabby," I said to my dog as she pawed my leg for attention. I was on the verge of throwing the paper in the bin when at that moment, Christine came in through the back door, her blonde hair hidden by a woolly hat. She was stamping her feet with cold, and the cheeks of her lovely face were pink.

"Brrrrr, it's freezing out there today. Barby, you're in the right place. Stay inside—I would if I could!" And with that she threw back her head and laughed.

"Barby, are you okay?" she asked, stopping her merriment to look me straight in the eye. "You look a bit odd . . ." Christine was very perceptive; it was why she was so good at nursing terminally ill patients and managing their grieving families. She had a kindness and firmness about her that people trusted, and she was used to seeing others when they were at their most vulnerable.

"Oh dear, does it show on my face? Well I've received a letter from my GP telling me to go for a bloody mammogram. I hate doctors, and I hate anything like this. I won't be going, of course."

Christine was already shaking her head from side to side before I'd finished speaking.

"Come on, Barby, you know you should go. What will you lose by going anyway?" she said, rather sternly. She didn't suffer any foolish behavior from me gladly.

"I knew you'd say that, which was why I wasn't going to tell you," I grumbled. "I will lose half a day at least, and there's so much that needs doing . . ." my voice trailed off. Even I knew I sounded weak.

Christine tutted, pulling off her hat and pulling out a chair at the table. She indicated for me to sit, which I did, reluctantly.

"Mammograms are really important, Barby, and you know it. There isn't anything going on here that we can't cope with while you're having the examination."

"What about the new stronger fencing for the pigs, some-one needs to supervise that," I replied, not quite catching Christine's eye.

"Dan can do that. Next objection?" she answered deftly.

"Well what about Gabby, how can I leave her? She'll get very upset. I've never left her for more than half an hour . . ."

"Diane could look after Gabby. She'll be fine with Harry

and Ben here as well. You know how much they protect her. Surely it's really important that you start the process of letting Gabby learn that if you go away, you come back?"

I couldn't argue with that.

"Alright, well, I'll think about it. That's all I'm going to promise. The appointment isn't for another few weeks, so I've got some time, dear. That's all I'm going to say about it." I knew I'd clammed up, but it was my decision to make.

Christine smiled. "You know best, Barby. If you're worried about it I'm more than happy to take you. Have a think and let me know."

I got up and excused myself, saying I had to go and sort the bread for the seagulls and assorted birds who all wanted feeding, but really I didn't like the feeling of "having" to do anything, and I wanted time to clear my head.

The days passed, and I tried not to think about the appointment. I've never been very good at doing the things I "have" to do. I'm a bit of a rebel at heart. It was one of the facets of my character that has enabled the sanctuary to prosper the way it has because I've always done things my way and not anyone else's, but it has also held me back from making decisions like these.

The mammogram was scheduled for 12:25 P.M. on January 30 at a mobile unit in Bexhill. At midday I was still fussing about at home, undecided about whether to go. Christine came inside, her blonde hair in pigtails, with Dee, her black-and-white collie, at her heels.

"Come on, Barby, I'm not waiting any longer. Please decide what you're doing. We've got just enough time to get there."

"I don't know. I really don't want to go, Christine. . . . I don't want to be mucked about by doctors. I've got a bad feeling about it," I said, frankly.

"You'll be fine," she reassured me. "You're fighting fit, and it's just routine. Come on, let's go together. It'll be nice to leave the sanctuary for an afternoon."

"Alright," I sighed in response, "but Diane will have to come in and look after my baby girl." I picked up the walkie-talkie.

"Di, can you leave what you're doing and come into the house? I need you to look after Gabby while I'm away for a couple of hours."

"Right you are," replied Di straight away.

Seconds later Di came in, wearing her muddy wellies, and sat down on the armchair nearest the doorway. I picked up Gabby, sniffed her lovely musky doggie scent, and handed her to Di.

"Look after her, won't you . . ."

"Of course I will," Di laughed. "Now go on or you'll be late."

I stroked Harry, pulling his long blonde ears gently, and patted Ben on his black head. Both dogs licked my outstretched hands and slumped themselves down on the rug next to Di, who was holding Gabby. I grabbed my fleece and vest from the hook and put on my boots. I didn't stand on ceremony. I would go in my work clothes and they'd have to like it or lump it.

"You're doing the right thing," said Christine sweetly and I nodded, saying nothing. I wasn't so sure, however.

While Gabby's progress was coming on in leaps and bounds, despite not yet making a proper barking noise, the spotlight had fallen on my well-being, and I didn't like it one bit.

I let Christine drive me the few miles to the hospital unit, saying barely a word all the way there. As it turned out, there was very little waiting time, and the examination was soon over, and I was told I'd receive the results in a couple of weeks.

"That's that, then. Good. I need to get back now. Gabby will be missing me. I've no idea whether she'll be okay without me being there. Harry will look after her as well as Diane, but it's me she wants . . ."

Separation anxiety is distressing both for the dog and owner, and so careful measures have to be introduced.

A pooch needs to be introduced to the fact of his or her owner's temporary disappearance in a gentle and staggered way. It is usual to start with a ten-minute separation if the dog is really anxious, building up to an hour or even a couple of hours to begin with. Rushing the method can backfire, and yet Gabby needed to learn that if I went away, I would come back to her again, and today had been the start of that process. I knew she was in safe hands with Di, but I hated the thought that Gabby would be upset by my absence.

We arrived back at the site after only a couple of hours away, but I virtually sprinted to the front room. On hearing my voice, Gabby skittered across the hallway to me, rolling on the floor in delight at my feet. Harry and Ben joined her, and in an instant I was surrounded by adoring hounds, a chaos of fur and wagging tails.

"Hello, darlings, hello, Gabby. Have you been a good dog

for Diane?" I crooned as I knelt down and hugged her. Gabby licked my face as I picked her up. Harry and Ben never seemed bothered by the attention I lavished on this newcomer. They sauntered off happily, checking out their bowls as they passed them in case dinner had been served early.

"Now, now, I've already had a wash today, stop that," I said, delighted by my welcome from Gabby.

"How was she?" I asked Di as soon as I came into the living room, still holding my precious pooch.

"I won't lie, Barby, she got very upset after about half an hour. She didn't make a noise but she kept pacing up and down, looking for you out of the window. She'll need a few more sessions of you leaving her with me before she gets used to it."

"Well it's about time I went back to my darts nights, I've been missing it," I said stoutly, looking back at my trophy cabinet. I must have won hundreds of shields and cups over the years, and they stood crammed together in my glass-fronted cabinet, winking in the light. I usually played with The Home Guard on Tuesdays, and if I could manage it, Barby's Critters on a Friday, both at the Sidley Working Mens' Club, but since Gabby had arrived I'd been reluctant to go out and leave her behind.

"Why don't you take her with you?" volunteered Di.

"That's not such a bad idea," I chuckled, wondering why I hadn't thought of that myself. "What do you think, Gabby, would you like to come to darts night on Friday with Mummy?" Gabby licked my face again and wagged her tail.

"That's her answer!" laughed Christine. We all smiled.

"Darts night it is then, Gabby. I can't wait to show you off to my other motley crew down there. You'll be the queen of the night, and will charm everyone, I'm sure of that," I said, kissing her soft fur.

Later that evening, I decided to take Gabby out for a short walk around the site. Every time I left it, I felt, upon my return, renewed gratitude for the startlingly beautiful place I was lucky enough to live in. Gabby trotted after me, sniffing every few paces, clearly becoming more and more used to the unfamiliar. We had only just reached the back field when Gabby started to become restless. She was sniffing the grass in a frenzied way, then she started circling. These were all signs she needed a poo. I stopped and waited, and lo and behold, she crouched in the way all dogs do and with a quivering back, she did her business outside for the very first time.

It wasn't the most glamorous of sights, but to me it was a revelation. Gabby had finally mastered the skill of pooing where she should—out in the fields as Mother Nature intended.

"Oh well done, girl, well done," I said after she had finished. Gabby ran over to me, clearly delighted by her own cleverness, and I chuckled as we carried on our walk.

What a strange day it had been.

Chapter 11
BAD NEWS

"Happy Birthday, Barby!" A sea of smiling faces greeted me as I entered the kitchen. I laughed out loud when I saw them all. The room was filled with balloons, and they'd made a banner that sagged slightly as it ran along the kitchen cupboards.

"Well, it was hardly a surprise, was it?" I laughed. "You lot have been out here whispering and making sandwiches for the last hour!"

"Come now, old lady, come and sit down and enjoy your birthday tea. We've all taken time off from the animals to celebrate with you. Don't you go having a grump with us," Di teased, grinning broadly.

All the gang were there: Diane, Harry, Dan, and several other volunteers who were in that day.

"Did I say I didn't like it?" I bantered back. "It's my party and I'll be grumpy if I want to! I'm only joking everyone, this is lovely, thank you all very much," I said, my eyes sweeping across the pile of food laid out. There were sandwiches, chips, cut-up salad bits, and, best of all, a dog bowl on the table filled with premium ham.

"You've laid a place for Gabby!" I exclaimed, clutching my heart. The thought touched me. "How lovely. Where's my guest of honor? There she is . . ." I bent over to pick up my dog, who was sniffing about at my feet as usual.

"We've even got her a paper hat," smiled Dan. He was right. There was a row of blue and pink cone-shaped hats for everyone, with a nice pink one by Gabby's bowl. I chuckled at the sight of that.

"Right, come and sit down. I'll make you a cuppa. Now how old did you say you were . . . ?" Di jested, bustling around to locate cups and the ceramic pot with the tea bags in.

"I'm not discussing my age. That's between God and my-self. You should never ask a lady how old she is!" I said with mock affront. I didn't really care who knew my age. I wasn't precious about getting older. The years tended to roll into one, and I rarely celebrated birthdays these days.

I spotted a beautiful bunch of flowers arranged on the side.

"Oh they're lovely," I exclaimed, going over to sniff them. I've never been very good at knowing which flowers are which, but they looked very pretty.

I lifted Gabby onto a chair, and popped the pink hat on her. She really looked so adorable. Everyone burst out laugh-ing. Gabby didn't seem to mind one bit. She nudged my hand with her nose, asking to be stroked, with the hat sliding to one side, making us laugh even harder.

But the day got even better, courtesy of my dog in her lop-sided hat, who had already wolfed down the treats laid in

front of her. She jumped down once she'd eaten enough birthday tea, and she rushed to greet Beany the dog when Fran
walked in from the fields.

"Have I missed anything?" he grinned, grabbing a vegan
roll.

Without a moment's hesitation, Gabby chased his tiny
Chihuahua, and the pair began tussling like old friends. I
watched with my mouth open, gawping at the change in my
beloved pooch.

"See, you got there in the end, Barby," someone said, and
all I could do was nod. It was an incredibly special moment,
and I felt like a proud parent.

The kitchen went quiet for a moment as everyone digested
the latest step forward lovable Gabby had taken, but they
soon switched attention to gossiping and general chatter. I
couldn't take my eyes off the dogs, though.

"Your cake, Barby!" Di said, carrying over a nice-looking
jam sponge with three lit candles wobbling on top of it, but
despite the sight, I just wanted to enjoy this moment, watching
Gabby play like a real, proper dog.

"Sorry dearest, I can't pull myself away. Look at them, look
at Gabby . . ." Di knew how much it meant to me. She paused
for a moment as she watched them, before placing the cake
in front of me.

"Blow them out and we can all get back to work, dear,"
she said in a matronly manner.

After they'd all gone and Beany had ambled off into another
room, I snuggled Gabby to me and told her what a brave and
wonderful dog she was.

"You learned to play at last. What a clever girl you are," I whispered into her fur. She smelled of outdoors, which in itself was an utter joy.

"I caught the ferrets, Barby," Dan announced a few days later as he marched in for his breakfast.

It was mid-morning and he was later than usual, so he'd buzzed in to me to say he was on his way. I was ladling out his customary baked beans as he took off his jacket and sat down at the wooden table in the center of my kitchen. Outside I could see the view stretching for miles over woodland and fields, and my small garden with bird feeders, piles of bread for the gulls, and a layer of frost that still sparkled although it was almost midday.

"How many were there in the end?" I asked. The ferrets had been living in one of the stables, and needed to be put into their own enclosure.

"There were six of them. They're in one of the big cat baskets just now but I'll find them a new home after I've eaten."

Dan's toast popped up out of the toaster, issuing an enticing smell.

"That's good news. And did you hear about the man with all those cats?" he asked, scraping margarine across one of the thick slices. Dan was vegan, along with most of the other volunteers. They were all animal lovers, some of whom had been activists in the past, but I wasn't sure I wanted to know about that.

"No, what's that?" I said, sipping my steaming hot cup of tea.

"A man called in saying he's got thirty-six cats that need rehoming."

I almost choked on my tea. "Thirty-six!"

Dan nodded. "And when I went over to his apartment— yes, he lives in an apartment," he added as he saw my jaw drop, "he had eight litter trays overflowing with you-know-what. Apparently he took in a couple of strays, didn't get them neutered, and bingo—kittens everywhere." Dan snorted with mirth as he swallowed.

I shook my head.

"I'm sorry, but that's just irresponsible," I sighed. "His heart was obviously in the right place, but for goodness sake, why didn't he get their bits chopped?"

Dan laughed out loud at that.

"I dunno. People eh? They go daft when it comes to animals."

Well, I couldn't deny that.

"I'll organize with Di where they'll all go. He says he only wants to rehome them with you, Barby—your reputation goes ahead of you."

I couldn't deny that, either, though I blushed at the compliment. Many people said they'd rather rehome with us because we were all in it just for the animals. Even though we'd become a charity, we didn't have the kind of structure with management and employees that other big organizations had. People knew that if they sent their animals here, or gave money to us, that everything was plowed back into caring for them.

Dan got up to leave, still chewing on a piece of toast.

"There's some mail on the side. The mailman came earlier while you were out feeding the pigs. Right, I'd better get back to work." And with that, Dan pulled on his fluorescent workman coat and headed outdoors. As he went, Gabby trotted past me, heading outside as well, though she was going through the dog door. I sat and beamed as I watched her go.

Her confidence had come on so much lately. Every day she went outside to do her business, morning and night, and on the mornings when Fran came in to the sanctuary from his apartment in Hastings, his little dog was deposited with me in the living room while he worked. Beany was a dear thing with bright little features and glossy jet black fur. Gabby was so improved that she would run up to the creature with delight, sniffing it, and the two of them had started to run after each other, playing "catch" and rolling around when one was victorious. It warmed my heart to see them.

"All you needed was time, and a lot of love," I said to myself, as Fran walked in with Beany at his heels.

"Right, I'm leaving him with you, I'm going to see about a pig that's been abandoned."

"Okay, dear," I called after Fran as he shot out.

Gabby returned from her business, and on seeing Beany, who had settled down in front of the lit fire, she showed her happiness by wagging her tail as the Chihuahua jumped up, and off they raced.

It was then I realized I hadn't opened my mail.

On the top of the pile sitting on the side by the coffee and tea containers, was a large white envelope with that all-too-familiar NHS logo on.

"What is it now?" I muttered, completely forgetting that they had said they would send me a follow-up letter after my mammogram. Life was so busy here that I had put it to the back of my mind.

The letter said very little. I had to go to Brighton Hospital to have a biopsy and get the mammogram results. I looked at the appointment date. It was only a few days away. *Hmm, that's very quick*, I thought to myself, a seed of worry settling somewhere in my mind. I was used to expecting long waits for NHS treatments.

I picked up the telephone and called my oldest friends, Elaine and Rob.

"Of course we'll take you. I'm sure it's nothing to worry about. Come on, Barby, chin up. You'll face whatever it is, you have to," Elaine said stoutly when I voiced my concerns at how rushed the process was proving to be.

Elaine, who was in her mid-forties and had gorgeous blonde hair, and her husband Rob, a kind man who had recently been laid off from his job printing the local newspaper, were my rocks. They were both strong-minded, independent people, a bit like me in that sense.

I'd met Elaine and Rob a couple of years previously, when they'd driven into my parking lot but had stayed in their car. Frowning at the CCTV image, and not recognizing their faces, I marched out to see what was going on. I'm only five foot tall, and quite petite, so it must have looked quite comical seeing me round on their car and demand they wind their window down.

"Can I help you? Why are you sitting in my parking lot?

Are you here to look at rehoming one of the animals?" I wasn't very polite.

Elaine and Rob hadn't seemed to mind. After exchanging a look between themselves, they rather cautiously wound their car window down and peered out at me.

"Actually we were looking to become volunteers, we were just checking we were in the right place . . ." Elaine replied, fixing me with her rather stern gaze.

"Oh well, that's alright then, come in," I huffed. Perhaps I knew I'd met my match in this woman!

By the time we'd all shared a cuppa together, the foundations for our friendship had been built. Elaine started volunteering in the shop, which was originally in Sackville Road, Bexhill, then moved to St Leonards Road in 2002.

What became clear early on was that Elaine would stand for no nonsense from me. I was such a fiery, emotional person that sometimes I needed people with a calm, wise persona around me. And I definitely needed that now. I felt comforted that my friends would be with me for this trip to the hospital, but anxious nonetheless.

The day of the appointment arrived. During the drive, I said very little, and when we parked up and entered the prefab building at the back of the hospital, we were greeted by a horrible silence. Women lined the room, all waiting for their scans or biopsies, all refusing to catch each other's eyes. There was a palpable sense of fear.

It was at that point that it hit me. Something *must* be wrong. Why else would I be here?

I'd left Gabby with Diane again, and at that moment I

longed for her to be there. Somehow that would make it, if
not okay, then better. I knew that everyone in that room was
fearing, or expecting, the worst. I was now one of them.

I was eventually called in after a tense hour-long wait.
Elaine smiled at me.

"Go in, Barby, you're a fighter. Don't let the side down."
I swallowed, but stood up and walked in. The next few minutes were a blur. The mammogram was repeated by a gentle
nurse, but before I could get dressed again, she said, "Miss
Keel, you'll have to go back to the waiting room again, I'm
afraid. We'll need to do a biopsy today, here at the hospital.
I'll need to mark where it's going to be so hold there, please."

The nurse produced a thick pen and she drew a cross on
my left breast. I didn't dare ask what she'd seen, though of
course I knew by now that it must be a lump of some description.

"You've marked me!" I said, half joking.

The nurse smiled at me. For a moment I thought I saw a
fleeting look of pity, but she turned away before I could be
sure.

My heart started to beat faster, and I escaped to the waiting
room gladly, if only just to see the familiar faces of my friends.

"We have to wait a bit longer, I'm afraid. I'm having a
biopsy."

Elaine nodded, but not before a brief glance passed between
her and Rob. We all knew this didn't look good. The next
half an hour was an agony of waiting. My palms were sweaty,
my throat dry. Elaine kept squeezing my arm, but I knew all
the time we were all thinking the same thing: cancer.

We were soon led to the part of the hospital where the biopsy was to take place, and presented with a cubicle for me to change into a gown.

"I'm not getting into one of those things," I erupted. Rob laughed, which helped ease the tension.

"Behave, Barby!" Elaine cut in. "My goodness, you're not a child. The nurses need you to do what you're told today." I smiled at that. When do I ever do what I'm told?

I chuckled. "Alright, I'm doing this for you, Elaine, and nobody else. I can't bear the sight of these gowns, they make people look *ill*." Even the nurse holding the cubicle curtain open for me laughed at that.

"Now, do what your friend says, and put the gown on, Miss Keel. I'll be back in a moment to check on you."

Ungraciously, I pulled the curtain shut, and within moments I had divested myself of my clothes and was handing them to Elaine, who had poked her head round the curtain.

"We'll see you soon, give them hell," she joked.

I was led into a large room surrounded with medical equipment. A rather stern woman was sitting at a computer with a large screen.

"Sit here, please. We're going to insert the needle to draw out some of the cells around this area here," she said, pointing to the screen as if to show me.

"I don't want to know what you're doing, and I don't want to see it, either," I said. "I just want you to get this done so I can go home to my dog as quickly as possible."

"Oh, you have a dog. What breed is it?" the woman asked.

She kept me talking about Gabby while the procedure was performed.

"She's a Lhasa Apso/Yorkie cross—and she's the loveliest thing you've ever clapped eyes on. I wouldn't be without her, I really wouldn't. In fact, the only thing that bothers me about coming here today is the guilt I feel at leaving her. She doesn't like it when I'm away . . ." I chatted away as the large needle was inserted into my breast, drawing out the fluids and cells. Part of me wasn't "with it" in the sense that I was in shock. Only days previously I'd been celebrating my birthday, surrounded by friends and colleagues without a care in the world, and now this. I felt utter disbelief mixed with a terrible fear that this could be it for me. I could be facing my toughest challenge yet and I wasn't sure I felt strong enough.

The whole procedure passed surprisingly quickly, and I barely felt anything, though they said the skin at the puncture point might bruise later.

"Okay, dear, all done, you can go back to your friends now," the nurse smiled.

I nodded and shuffled back, but there was no one in the waiting area.

I stood there for what felt like hours, naked apart from the gown, while a draft went up the back of my ludicrous outfit.

When I eventually saw Elaine and Rob walking down the corridor, I shouted to them. "I'm standing here with my arse hanging out, flapping in the breeze, while you're off enjoying yourselves! I want my bleedin' clothes!"

"Well it's obvious your sense of humor is intact," Elaine

roared back, collapsing with laughter. "You told us you'd be twenty minutes, so we went and got a coffee and did the crossword."

"The bloody crossword!" I shrieked.

I was just about to continue with yet more banter in response, when the nurse came back, telling me I had to wait to see the consultant.

"You mean we're still not finished here?" I retorted.

"Calm down, Barby, of course you've got to see the head honcho. Now why don't you get dressed and we'll get you a cuppa before the appointment," Elaine said, taking charge of the situation.

Soon I was sipping tea from a vending machine while we waited in yet another room, this one being more like a corridor lined with plastic chairs.

We didn't have to wait long. My name was called by yet another nurse, but this time she asked, "Do you want your friend to come in with you?" I looked up at the young woman and shook my head. Why would I need a friend with me?

"I just want to get this over and done with," I said again, and the nurse nodded.

"Come this way."

The consultant was an Asian man with a rather officious manner.

"You know why you're here, Miss Keel," he said as a statement rather than a question. "You have a malignant tumor, I'm awfully sorry."

There was silence, then the sound of me taking in a great breath.

Remember to breathe . . . I told myself, my head spinning.

"Do you need some water?" The consultant, a man in his fifties with glasses, looked at me now with genuine concern.

I shook my head. Still no words would come out. I had a brief thought that this must be how Gabby felt when she wanted to bark. The shock. The silence. The struggle for breath, and for sound. Bless her. She couldn't help it. I saw that so clearly in that terrible moment. I kept asking her to bark and yet it must be caught in her throat, just as my reaction to the terrible news was.

I felt numb. Utterly shaken. I couldn't register the room, the man in front of me leaning across the table. I could only think of Gabby, and the sanctuary, and what the hell would happen to all of it if I died.

"Do you want me to ask the nurse to get your friend?" he said, breaking my bubble. I managed to nod in reply.

Seconds later, Elaine was beside me. She held my right hand, and said, "Whatever happens, we'll face it together." I appreciated the sentiment. She was my closest friend, but deep down I wasn't so sure. I knew that I'd have to face this alone, and the thought frightened me more than anything in my whole life so far.

Chapter 12

BREAKING POINT

This can't be happening...
   This isn't real...
I don't have cancer...
I DON'T have cancer... I have cancer...
I have CANCER...
Oh my God, I DO have cancer... What if I die?
I'm too young to die...
Who will look after Gabby if I die?
Who will run the sanctuary when I'm gone? Why me?
God, help me, please...

The voices were stuck in my head and just went round and round, in a seemingly endless spiral, much like a goldfish swimming round and round all day without moving forward.

The consultant, Dr. Allen, continued, "But you are lucky, Miss Keel, if that's a word we can use here. It's an A1 tumor, which means you can't get smaller than that. We've caught it in good time."

I could see his lips move, but the words just refused to

register in my brain. I opened my mouth, expecting words to come out, but nothing happened. Fear rose in my belly like a great serpent. I felt sick, dizzy, strange. The room and the doctor seemed to float in front of me.

"Barby's going into shock, I think she might faint . . ." came Elaine's voice from what seemed like a million miles away.

In a funny way, that helped to steady me.

"No, no, I'm fine," I replied. "I just need a moment—and some water, please."

The consultant buzzed for the nurse, and a few seconds later she returned with the drink. My hand shook as I put the white plastic cup to my mouth. I can still remember the sensation of the cold water against my tongue, the feel of the plastic rim against my lips; everything was so heightened, so bizarre. I knew I'd never forget that moment, that point where my life, my health, everything I knew about myself, crashed and collided into this diagnosis.

If you'd asked me to stake my life on my health I wouldn't have hesitated for a moment. I was a fit old bird. I carried bales of hay. I dragged sacks of animal feed. How could I possibly have cancer when I could do all those things and more? It didn't make sense. Nothing made sense. I felt my body sag like a burst balloon.

I had a thousand questions, yet I couldn't say a word. Despite the water, my tongue felt dry on my lips.

"Barby, are you okay? Come on love, we're here for you, we'll get through this, I promise you," Elaine said, gripping my hands. They felt icy-cold against her warmth.

"What now?" was all I could eventually say.

The consultant's face was grave. "You'll need to have surgery, and then you'll need to take a drug called tamoxifen, which you'll take for the rest of your life. Considering your age and general fitness, I would expect a full recovery with all those treatments combined together . . ."

"Stop there," I interrupted him.

"I understand I've got the C-word, and that I need surgery. I'll be guided by you as a health professional, but I won't be having chemo, and I won't take any medication." At that moment I knew that I couldn't stand any more intervention. I felt it with every fiber of my body—as sure about it as anything I'd ever felt in my life. I knew I'd have to have surgery—that I understood—but that was where I drew the line. My sudden clarity centered me, steadied me.

I was thinking of a dear friend from Eastbourne who, years earlier, had undergone chemotherapy. She had lost all her hair and found the process very traumatic.

I recalled how sick she was in between doses and how frightened it made me, even at the time. The surgery would be invasive enough, I couldn't face going through all that on top of it.

"Miss Keel . . ." the consultant began, but I stopped him again.

"Dr. Allen, I appreciate your help but it is my body and this is my decision."

I looked over at my friend and nodded my head. She could see the look of fierce determination on my face. Even Elaine wasn't foolish enough to try to change my mind. She knew that when I'd made a decision I didn't deviate, I didn't step back. If I'd said no, then no was what I meant.

"Alright, then, Barby, whatever you think is best. You can always think about it when we're away from here," she said, squeezing my hand as she spoke.

"As I've said, I've made my decision. Surgery is okay but nothing else."

My face must have looked extremely stern as Dr. Allen nodded back at me, mutely. "You are risking the cancer returning by not doing the full treatment program, but I understand how you feel. I've had patients in the past decide the same, even though I'd advise you not to."

"Doctor, please tell me about the surgery. Will I be in hospital long? How long will it take to recover? And is there any chance that I won't come through the procedure?"

Questions were coming thick and fast now as the impact of the news started to sink in.

The consultant leaned back in his chair and flicked his eyes to his computer screen.

"It should just be a couple of days in the hospital. You should only need keyhole surgery and six stitches, so the recovery time will be shorter than a standard operation. As for not coming out of the anesthetic, there is always the risk, Miss Keel, but this surgery is vital.

"Do you have anything more you want to ask me at this stage?"

I had too many questions whirring about in my mind but I suddenly felt exhausted. It had been a difficult, and unexpectedly long, day and all I wanted to do was get home and cuddle my dog again. I shook my head.

"Okay, we'll be in touch very soon, Miss Keel—we will write to you again with the date for your procedure. In the meantime, try not to worry."

Easy for him to say, I thought, as I shook his hand before leaving the room. I'm not sure how my legs carried me as we walked out into that long corridor, where we saw Rob half rise from his seat, his face white because he had guessed. He *knew* what the bad news was. How could he not?

"Is it . . . ?" He stumbled at the "c"—the start of the dreadful word that now hung over me.

Elaine must've nodded as Rob looked at her and then put his arm around me.

"Come on, Barby, you're in the best possible hands, and no illness will ever get the better of you, old girl, it wouldn't dare."

I had to smile at that.

"You cheeky sod! I'm not that old!" I countered.

"Back to her old self already. Well that bodes well for a full recovery, eh, Barby?" added Elaine but I didn't have the heart to joke about it.

I barely registered walking along the long corridors of the hospital, the long white stretches, the bright pictures hung to make patients feel better. People shuffled past me, patients in those dreadful gowns pulling along their bags of IV liquids attached to them, but I barely saw them or the surgeons walking past, their faces muzzled by white masks, their plastic clogs making sly squeaking noises on the linoleum. It was a place of medical sanctity and human vulnerability, and I knew I would be returning as a patient, an ill person, a person with cancer.

"Now come on, Barby," Elaine said, "I'm not going to have any nonsense from you. If anyone can face this, then it's you, my dear. You're a born survivor. You're a fighter, and, my goodness, you have the fiercest temper of any woman I've ever met, and that will stand you in very good stead to get through this."

She squeezed my arm. I was being propped up by both my friends. We walked arm in arm together, making our way back out to the parking lot. By the time we got to the car, I was seething with rage, and I wasn't even sure why.

I burst out, "I just want to see Gabby. I don't want to think about this anymore. I don't understand, Elaine. Why me? Why has this bloody well happened to me?"

I felt the anger rise like bile in my throat. I wanted to shout or pummel a pillow, anything to release the buildup of tension from the day.

"This is not fair. It's not fair. So many people are relying on me. So many animals need me. What will they do if I'm not here to look after them?" I heard a sob form at the back of my throat. I felt like a child getting upset at the way the world was.

"Now then, Barby, you're not alone. Thousands of people get news like this every day. It's not your fault, there's nothing you could have done differently to prevent this. It's just how life is sometimes," Elaine soothed me as Rob drove. She sat in the back with me, protecting me in her own way.

"I'd better phone the sanctuary. They'll be waiting for news, and we've been a long time," I cut in.

"And I want to see how Gabby has managed without me, bless her," I added as I dialed the number on Elaine's mobile phone.

The number rang a couple of times before someone, a female voice, picked up.

"Hello, Animal Sanctuary."

"Oh Christine, I'm glad it's you. I'm on my way back. Don't say anything to the others, but it's not good news."

"Oh dear, Barby, I hope you're okay. Alright, I won't say anything. How long will you be? Gabby has been pining, I'm afraid. She doesn't like you being away this long."

"Well, tell her that Mummy will be home soon." I rang off, suddenly feeling nauseous at the thought of facing everyone and telling them my news. All I wanted was my darling hound in my arms and the warm comfort of her doggie smell and soft fur against me.

Less than an hour later, we pulled into the sanctuary parking lot. Without a word, we all got out and headed through the main gate, making sure to shut it behind us.

Peter the Peacock had just strutted into view at the far end of the yard, but even the sight of his beauty held no magic for me today. What would I say to all my loyal helpers? How could I form the words to describe what was happening? I felt at a loss. However, being back in familiar surroundings was already acting like a salve. I started feeling a little more like my old self as we opened the front door and went inside.

I reached the kitchen first, and stopped to see the room full of the day's volunteers, all waiting for our return at the kitchen table. They stood up and looked at me.

Christine was there, her face pale. Diane was there, too, as well as William, Dan, and several other staff and helpers, who all looked at me expectantly.

"Close your ears," I ordered.

"Why, Barby?" Christine said in her lovely gentle voice.

"Because I'm going to scream!

"I HAVE CANCER . . ." I yelled as loudly as I could, my voice high-pitched with fear.

Then I broke down into the sobs that had been threatening me all day. I wept and wept, crumpling into someone's arms, I think it was Christine, who guided me onto a kitchen chair, where I sat like a bag of potatoes.

I cried harder than I'd ever cried before, not caring one jot that so many people were witnessing my moment of vulnerability. I had never broken down so completely in all my life, but I couldn't stop myself. It was as if all the tears I'd ever saved up, that were dammed up somewhere in my subconscious, were now flooding out of me.

I felt arms hold me, a cup of hot tea placed into one hand, a rub on the back by someone else. Everything fell away from me in that moment, and I just needed to weep until it was all out and I could start the process of coming to terms with all this.

Then I felt a movement by my leg. Then a sniff, and another, and a wagging tail buffeting my leg as I sat there. Instinctively I knew it was Gabby and I bent down and lifted her onto my lap, nuzzling my face in her fur.

"Oh, Gabby, there you are, my darling girl. I have missed you so much today. And what a day it's been. I wished I could've taken you there . . ."

The little dog turned her face up to me, her eyes like deep wells, soaking into me. I looked at her and she licked my nose. She knew. I could tell that she knew I was struggling more than I ever had before. Our bond was so complete, so natural and deep, that she appeared just at the right moment. She helped me to dry my tears, to lick away the rivulets of salt that had run down my face, and help me start to feel better, one doggie cuddle at a time.

Later, when everyone had decided that I was over the worst and they started drifting off to finish the jobs that needed doing at the end of the day, I gathered Gabby to me and took her off to bed.

"We'll have an early night. I'm feeling very tired, and I think I'll need to catch up on my sleep before the surgery and all the nonsense that lies ahead," I told her.

Gabby looked at me, her head cocked to one side, as if she understood every word.

"What a clever dog you are. You know there's something going on, don't you?"

In response, my fluffy mutt snuggled closer to me as we settled on the bed.

I lay there for hours, listening to the sounds of the sanctuary: the goats baaa-ing for their evening feed, the horses whinnying in the back fields. I could hear the sounds of the birds as they roosted for the night, the low crows of the roosters and the hens as they, too, made way for nightfall.

Every now and then, someone would knock on my door and ask "Are you okay?," "Do you need anything?" and my answer was always the same: "No, thank you, dear, I just need a bit of peace and quiet."

I never got much time to reflect during my busy days, and I think at that point, probably the lowest in my life, I suddenly realized how much I'd achieved setting up the shelter. I suddenly saw what a gargantuan effort it all was: feeding, watering, housing, and taking care of so many animals of so many descriptions.

At that point we had horses, donkeys, ponies, pigs, goats, sheep, dogs, cats, rabbits, seagulls, peacocks, gerbils, hens, chickens, cockerels, geese, and ducks.

For once in my frenetic life, I got the chance to see what an important job we all did in looking after these poor animals, saving them from being abandoned, beaten, discarded, or put down. All the animals that lived here owed their lives and well-being to the people who worked here and the many supporters who kept us going day to day, week to week, year to year with their donations of money or food. It was a powerful recognition, and I felt the magic of it, and how humble it made me feel. It had all started with me and my dad and a few animals that locals rehomed with me. We had just four acres, those ramshackle, leaking RVs, and a field or two with a bit of fencing and a few donations of animal feed. I could hardly believe that I had built all this up from such small beginnings into what the sanctuary was today: a thriving shelter that helped any animal that came our way with properly built enclosures, gleaming new kennels, a cattery and hospital, a section for FIV cats, and land and pens for the farm animals. We gave people new loves in the form of rescue dogs and cats. We helped match people and animals—bringing joy and contentment to humans and creatures alike in the process. I'd achieved a lot, and it wasn't often I allowed myself to see that.

As I lay there, long into the night, I thought about those years since 1971, the struggles and challenges, and the fun and laughter, and I realized in that moment that whatever happened with this cancer, I didn't regret a single second of my life. Cancer could throw its worst at me, and I was more than ready to face it—with my beloved Gabby at my side.

Chapter 13

HOSPITAL

"Barby, are you there?" Dan appeared behind me as I fed chunks of bread to the Saddleback pig in the farm animal enclosure.

I had a soft spot for pigs. They were rather civilized animals, being so clean with their toilet habits and sleeping arrangements. They also looked very funny as they ate their food, bits spewing out as they munched, their mouths curling up so that they always looked like they were smiling.

We currently had a new pig that had come to us from a farmer who needed to sell his land and had contacted us to see if we could take him.

The unnamed British Saddleback pig had arrived and was a handsome beast with distinctive black markings covering his face, ears, and rear end, with a pink stripe in the middle over his belly. I was trying out new names for him as I fed him, his comical face peering up at me in the hope of more bread. Gabby was at my feet as usual, sniffing at the air.

Spring had arrived, and, as I leaned over the fencing I could feel the April sunshine on my back. The sanctuary was stirring into life again after the winter chill. The early spring shoots were appearing on the trees, the lush promise of bountiful green foliage, and the birds had started singing again, preparing for their mating season. The sky, which had been an overcast gray for most of March, was now blue with a fresh wind that still made me shiver in the early mornings.

"Bacon . . . that's a good name, isn't it? Or how about Sidney? Do you like that one?"

I laughed as the pig nuzzled my hand through the stout fencing. Pigs are huge beasts and are extremely strong, so all of our residents had robust pens even though, if they chose, they could knock almost anything down and get away. Our pigs knew they were on to a good thing staying here with us, with regular meals, treats, and lots of tickling between the ears.

"Barby, I need to speak to you," said Dan as he marched up behind me.

"I've been trying to think of a name for this one. What do you think of Bacon?" I chuckled, turning to my farm manager, but when I saw Dan's face I almost recoiled. His normally cheerful demeanor was gone, and he looked very pale. He pushed back his glasses as he was wont to do when he felt uncomfortable.

"What is it? You've got a face like a ghost. Come on, spit it out? It isn't Di or Christine, is it?" I said, suddenly startled.

"No, no, it's not them but something has happened . . .

Barby, I'm so sorry to have to tell you this, but it's Brian, the man who gave us the tree and all those rosebushes last week."

Dan's kind face was drawn, and I could tell instantly that this was bad news indeed.

"He was only here last Sunday. What happened, Dan?" I leaned against the post, trying to prepare myself for the shock I knew was coming.

"He killed himself," Dan said. I heard myself gasp.

"He killed himself?" I repeated, foolishly, my brain playing catchup with my mouth.

"Yes, he ordered the tree and brought in the rosebushes, said good-bye to everyone as normal, then he went home and took an overdose of sleeping tablets . . ."

"Just like his sister Wendy," I replied, my voice trailing off as I recalled her. She was a lady in her forties, a gently spoken, quiet woman who also visited here regularly, then one day she took herself off after their mother's death and ended her life, though I didn't know the details.

People could only take so much. We all had our limits—I understood that, although it had been a great shock at the time. It was just so terribly sad that Brian, only in his early forties, had reached his, too. He was a regular at the sanctuary, coming every Sunday during the spring and summer months—I had always got the impression that his life was rather lonely. We had quite a few "regulars" who showed up come rain or shine. We provided a place in which everyone could belong, the only condition for entry being a love of animals. People often led quite isolated lives, especially those who had never married or had children. We attracted quite a few lost souls, as I liked to call them.

There was no judgment here, no barriers dividing us. I didn't care if you had two pounds or two million pounds—and neither did anyone else. I had members of my motley crew who wore diamond rings while cleaning out the rabbit hutches, and who wore ruinously expensive wellies while shoveling soiled hay from the horses' stables. No one cared, least of all me. It was what was in your heart that mattered, that was my belief in life, and many people said that when they walked through the gate into the sanctuary, they felt they were at "home" in a way many had never felt before in their lives. That is the power of caring for animals—as I've said before, they heal us in so many more ways than we can ever care for them. By looking after them, we are helped, maybe even saved. But time had run out for Brian.

"What could we have done? Could we have helped him more? Could we have done more? Is this our fault?" I stammered, wiping away a tear. I reached down to stroke Gabby without thinking. I needed the comfort that touching her gave me, the feeling that anchored me to my land and my heart.

"There was nothing we could've done, Barby, you know that. He had lost his sister and mother. It was tragic, and he was obviously very lonely. Sometimes we can't help people, it's as simple as that." Dan stopped and followed my gaze out to the fields. Everything was peaceful and quiet except for the sounds of the animals going about their business, thankfully oblivious to the scope of human suffering we each had to contend with.

"We'll plant those rosebushes today and say a few words over them. We'll also plant the tree prominently in the sanctuary and call it Brian in memory of him," I decided.

"Then when it grows it will provide shade for our visitors and his life won't have been in vain."

I was struggling to speak, my voice overcome with emotion. I hadn't known the man well, but he had been a friend to my motley crew, and he deserved our respect and a proper send-off.

I paused. It was an odd feeling, honoring the life of a man who had been so desperate to leave this mortal plane. I was fighting for my life in the only way I knew how. *My* way, on *my* own terms, but fighting nonetheless. I couldn't fathom how someone could want to end it. I had so much to lose, so many animals and people who needed me. Still, I'd been sent my date for the surgery, only days away, and was doing my very best not to think about it. I hadn't packed yet—and I hadn't sorted out who would be responsible for looking after Gabby in my absence. Luckily I had so much to do at the sanctuary that I fell into bed exhausted each night and fell asleep, which was exactly how I wanted it to be.

There was no point in worrying about the operation or dwelling on my mortality. I didn't have time for that. If I did get a bit maudlin I had my friend Elaine to tell me to stop fussing and get on with life. I knew I was blessed, but I also knew I wasn't ready to die yet—and the possibility of it angered me more than anything else.

I was convinced Gabby knew I was going away for a few days as she never left my side, only to do her business and to eat. She was like my shadow. I didn't need to look out for her,

I knew as I walked across the site that she was always right beside me. I couldn't express how grateful I was that this little dog had come into my life. The comfort and love she gave me was priceless, and I relied on it more and more as the dreaded day approached.

Two weeks later in May, the morning finally arrived that I was due to leave for Eastbourne Hospital, where the operation was being performed. I had arranged for Di to look after Gabby while I was away, and so I'd given her a long list of instructions, which she waved away with one hand, grinning, "Barby, Gabby will be fine with me. She can sleep on my bed, and I've got her toys and food bowl. I know she likes ham for her main meal and only the best dried dog food in the evening. She won't starve, and she'll be here waiting for you when you get back . . . and she'll be with Harry and Ben, they always take good care of her . . ."

"That's not the point, Diane," I grumbled in response. "I know you'll do everything right, it just won't be the same for her with me being away. This bloody cancer. Why did it have to happen now I've got Gabby? I'm more worried about leaving her than I am going in for this bloody op!"

That wasn't strictly true. For the last few nights, I'd lain awake, listening to the night sounds at the shelter, but unable to find any rest myself. Endless questions encircled me, like swallows at dusk, yet never seeming to settle.

What if I die, God?

Who will look after Gabby and the other animals? Who will run the sanctuary if I'm not here?

As a way of preempting anything untoward, I'd come to a

hasty arrangement with the sanctuary charity, selling them my land and the bungalow for the princely sum of £1, so that the charity owned everything. We had drawn up the papers at a charity trustee meeting after I'd received the news about my biopsy confirming the worst. If I died, there'd be no wrangles over my will, no problems at all. I had sat at the kitchen table, the light fading from the sky, with the forms in front of me. I'd bought this land thirty-two years ago, and there I was, about to sign away my life's work. How had it come to this? But as I watched the sky darken, I felt both sadness and an emotion bordering on relief; this way, at least I knew that whatever happened, the animals would be safe and secure. Everything I'd done since setting up home here was for animals—and this decision was no different. My pen swept across the page. It was done. I owned nothing except for the clothes I was wearing, my collection of meerkats and wind chimes, and my dogs. I hadn't expected to feel so free, so strangely lightened at a time I thought I'd only feel loss. I'd built up the sanctuary, and now it was time to prepare for the next generation to take over, though hopefully that wouldn't be for years to come.

Elaine and Rob arrived early to drive me to the hospital, Rob taking my overnight bag, which I'd hastily packed the night before, out to the car while I said good-bye to Di, Christine, Dan, and a few others who were in that day. I managed not to cry until I had to cuddle my dog for possibly the last time. I almost couldn't hand her back to Di.

Gabby was warm and soft in my arms, and I buried my face against her neck. Her eyes when they looked up at me were so knowing, it was almost as if she understood that I was going somewhere important. I don't know who looked more sorrowful, me or her, but Gabby sensed something was amiss and started making little distressed noises like small, high-pitched moans. I'd all but given up hope she'd ever bark.

"You'll be fine, and I'll be home soon and I'll be right as rain," I said, as much to reassure myself as the dog.

"You don't know what I've survived so far, little one. I've been shot at by a German bomber. I was almost bombed as a child, and saw my home blown to smithereens. I even survived my mum, and she gave me a difficult childhood, I can tell you. There was no love from her, so I can face this and fight it, okay, Gabby?"

"Come on, Barby, you'll be fine," Dan said kindly. He had appeared through the back door, and could see I was at the point of refusing to go, despite my strong words. Inside I felt as weak and scared as a child.

"What's all this? Stop those tears this instant, and get a move on. You'll be back in a couple of days then you can enjoy being looked after for once," Elaine said stoutly, and I managed a weak smile as I handed my dumpling back to my farm manager and let myself be guided out of my home.

I didn't look back as I left the site, the familiar clunk of the metal gate closing behind me, the barks from the kennels audible from behind the parking lot. I knew if I turned round I'd just start crying again. I don't think I said a word all the way to the hospital.

Elaine and Rob chatted, passing round mints and asking about the volunteers, but I didn't have the heart to respond.

I was afraid—I knew that now. I was as scared as I'd ever been about anything in my life. I didn't know what lay ahead, and I didn't know when I'd see my beloved dogs again, *if* I'd see them again. . . . Poor Harry and Ben didn't get much of a look-in when it came to the swell of my affections, but neither seemed to mind that Gabby held such a special place in my heart. They both still came for walks with me most days, and, of course, they slept by my bedside though it was only Gabby now who slept up on the bed with me. Even I balked at the thought of three dogs lying on top of me each night!

It was Gabby I was most worried about. Harry and Ben were comfortable living at the sanctuary, and I honestly thought that if anything did happen to me, anyone there could take them on, and they'd be perfectly happy. I knew that wouldn't be the case with Gabby. Our bond was so strong now that I knew she'd suffer terribly without me, and that knowledge filled me with anguish.

At the hospital I was directed to my ward and told to wait in the dayroom, as there was still someone in the bed that had been allocated to me.

We waited there for most of the day, sipping revolting vending-machine tea and flicking through well-thumbed copies of celebrity magazines that I wasn't interested in. I hated leaving the bubble of my world, the everyday problems and challenges we had looking after so many animals. I couldn't have cared less who was marrying whom or who had divorced someone else—I was more worried about the rabbits that needed their claws trimmed, or the pregnant ewes being given to us by the owners of a smallholding.

"It isn't fair. None of this is fair," I muttered as I paced the small sunlit room with its wipe-clean chairs and single television set in the corner.

"Now, Barby, what have I told you—don't upset yourself," said Elaine, overhearing me, even though she'd appeared to be engrossed in the photos of a mansion belonging to a famous couple.

I looked over to her and shrugged. Elaine tutted and carried on reading, her blonde bob catching the light.

"Why don't I go and get us a sandwich?" said Rob, rising off his chair, probably trying to make the peace. He was a slim and rather tall man with a friendly face and quiet manner.

"Good idea. Cheese and salad for me, please," replied Elaine. "Barby, what do you want?"

"I'm not allowed to eat. I'm meant to be going down for bleedin' surgery today, but nothing seems to be happening," I huffed.

Elaine and Rob exchanged a look. They knew me well enough to know I was all bluster, and that my irritability often covered deep-seated fear.

"Sorry love, of course you can't. Perhaps we'll eat later, Rob, eh."

"Why me?" I said again, for the thousandth time.

"Darling, why not you?" was all Elaine said in response, arching her brows. "None of us gets away with being human. Now look, here's the nurse, be polite and remember your manners, dearest."

I giggled at that. A nurse had indeed arrived. She was a youngish woman with brown hair and a nice smile.

"We're ready for you, Miss Keel, come this way . . ."

When, finally, I was changed and ready, and the porters had come to wheel me and my rather cumbersome bed down to the operating theater, I said, "See you soon" to my friends, and they waved me down the length of the ward.

I lay on that bed, watching the ceiling move, the strip lights streaking along the corridors, the awkward silences from the porters, who both smelled strongly of cigarette smoke. I'd never smoked in my life, and the irony of having cancer when all around me people were literally courting the condition didn't fail to strike me.

It was then, as I was lying back on the trolley, being wheeled to the operating theater, I began to pray. My mouth moving in silent prayer, I asked my God to love and care for all of my animals and my motley crew.

If anything happens to me, take care of them all please God, especially Gabby.

Please keep Gabby safe. Keep all of them safe . . . but please, please get me through this operation safely. I couldn't bear the thought of my dog feeling abandoned again, and she would feel that way if I died and left her.

I knew there was a risk of dying with any surgical procedure. It was a reality—and one I needed to acknowledge. In those few precious minutes before the bed was shunted into the lift and taken down into the bowels of the building to the operating room, I thought of all the animals and people in my care, the endless paperwork, the rules and regulations concerning the sanctuary, its processes and its ways, and my place so firmly at the heart of it all. Who would take it all on if I died? It wasn't clear to me, and the thought terrified me.

These were difficult questions and I didn't have the answers. Deep down, I knew that my team would carry on my work if anything happened, but the thought of leaving the little dog who had only been with me for eight months was simply too painful to bear.

As we reached the open doors of the operating room, I felt my chest tighten, my fears making me short of breath, my worries crowding into my head. I was panicking now. I wanted to get up and run away as fear and dread engulfed me.

"Will it hurt?" I heard myself say.

A woman with a surgical mask and cap on leaned over and looked at me.

"You've already got a cannula in your arm. That's good. Okay, I'm going to inject you now. It won't hurt at all. Just count to ten, Barby. Is it okay to call you Barby?"

"Yes, it's okay, but . . ." I started to reply. I wanted to tell her I'd changed my mind and wouldn't be having the operation after all, but my head felt sluggish, my words not quite leaving my mouth.

"Just count to ten. Can you do that for me, Barby, please . . ."

"1 . . . 2 . . . 3 . . ."

My thoughts subsided as the anesthesia surged through my veins, doing its work, and I felt myself sinking into blessed blackness.

Chapter 14

PERFECT MOMENT

"She's awake, I can see her eyelids fluttering," came a voice from overhead.

"She's moving. Hey Barby, we're all here. Your stepdaughter Sharon is here, and she wants to make a fuss of you. Wakey wakey, sleepyhead . . ." It was Elaine. I felt myself smiling.

My eyes opened, and the first person I saw was indeed Sharon, with her long dark hair, glamorous clothes, and high heels. She wasn't strictly my stepdaughter, as I was never actually married to her father, a former partner of mine, but we always thought of ourselves as family. Sharon, who was in her late thirties, and I had a close bond. Even though my relationship with her father had ended some years ago, Sharon and I still went out for dinner most weeks and I regularly delighted in her company.

I'd first known Sharon when she was a ten-year-old with blonde pigtails and the most adorable smile. I have never been one of those people who melts at the sight of children, preferring animals, but Sharon was different. We'd bonded the minute she introduced herself to me one weekend five years after I'd moved to Freezeland Lane. I'd split up from Les by then and had met someone else, although the memories of that relationship weren't good, so I never spoke about him. Meeting Sharon was the best thing to come out of that situation.

I knew very little about her mum, and I didn't want to know. I felt it was none of my business, and so when my partner went off at weekends to visit Sharon, he went with my blessing. It was a big moment to finally meet her, but one we both handled with customary humor. I liked Sharon straight away. She wasn't fussy or difficult, and she didn't back off from my silly mutts who lolled over to greet her; in fact, from the get-go she made me laugh.

"You look funny," she had said, and I burst out laughing.

"Well, I didn't expect you to say that, young lady. Why don't you get changed and come and help me with the pigs? Perhaps you'll end up looking funny, too," I replied, grinning.

That was that. We were firm friends from that day onward, so I was happy that it was her lovely face that greeted me as I came round from the anesthetic.

"There she is . . . hello, Barby, now don't move a muscle, we're going to look after you, it's about time you had someone take care of you for a change . . ."

Sharon winked at me as she carried on chatting away, arranging flowers in the vase that sat on the table at the end of my bed.

I tried to watch her, but the room suddenly seemed too bright, and I tried to lift myself up as the first waves of nausea hit me.

"Whoa there, Barby, don't move, I said! You've only just come round from your operation, you need to lie back and rest. You're not ready to sit up." Sharon's voice was warm but firm, and I sank back into the pillows.

I didn't feel any pain yet, though my left side was stiff. I felt woozy, and the whole room seemed to spin, but I was determined to sit up, and ignoring her advice, I tried again.

I felt hands hold my shoulders as Elaine stood up and gently pushed me back down into bed.

"But I want my teeth! Bring me my false teeth, I want to put them in," I bellowed.

The room went quiet for a split second, then I was greeted by gales of laughter.

"Oh, Barby, is that all you're worried about?" said Elaine in between giggles. "Bless you, you've had a major operation, you're covered in wires and surrounded by machines, and you're worried about your teeth!"

"I want my bleedin' false teeth . . . I can't let you lot see me without them," I cried again, feeling bile rise into my chest. It was true. I was very self-conscious about my teeth—or lack of them—and it made me feel even worse to think they were languishing in a cup of water somewhere rather than making me look respectable, at the very least.

"Anyway, how's Gabby? How's my darling girl? Is Diane

looking after her properly?" I managed to say, though rolling the words around my overly spacious mouth felt very strange. I didn't usually talk to anyone, except my dogs, until I had my teeth in.

"She's fine, don't worry about Gabby. She follows Di around everywhere, but she keeps sniffing your chair and bed. It's obvious that she knows you're missing, but she's not pining all day." Elaine didn't quite look me in the eyes as she spoke, which even in my altered state, I picked up on.

"Are you sure about that? You're not fibbing to me, are you?" I tried to give my words some impact, but I was feeling very weak all of a sudden and very dizzy.

"Please, don't worry, Barby. Di knows what she's doing. Of course Gabby misses you, it's natural, but she's not suffering. It's best if you concentrate on getting better so that you can get home to her."

Elaine's face was stern now, and I recognized the steely quality in her that I admired. She would say no more on the subject, and I respected her for that. Anyway, I had my own immediate concerns to face.

"Oh, I feel a bit strange, I don't like this one bit, and what's all this hanging out of me? I look like I'm a bloody robot," I said with a wail, looking down at the wires that protruded from underneath my left armpit. There was a huge dressing over my left breast, and I was starting to feel the soft thud, thud of the pain seeping through the painkillers.

It was Elaine who soothed me this time.

"Now then, Barby, the nurse will be coming round to check

on you, and you promised to be good while you were in hospital."

"I did no such thing!" I replied rather grandly for a woman strapped into a hospital bed by wires and tubes. A machine beeped next to me as if to remind me that it was there, too.

"What *is* all this stuff? Didn't the consultant say I was having keyhole surgery and six stitches . . . Well, this doesn't look like bloody keyhole surgery at all . . ."

"Don't upset yourself," countered Elaine, holding my right hand. Hers felt so warm against my cold skin, I momentarily lost my train of thought.

"Don't speak, Barby, you sound very croaky, that'll be the effect of the anesthetic. Just let yourself be looked after. You've had a rough evening, and the nurse will be along any minute . . ."

"Bring me my teeth, Elaine, I'm not bloody seeing anyone till I've got me chompers in . . ."

Elaine smiled and tutted, much as if she was talking to an irate child.

"Dearest Barby, you are an obstinate, stubborn woman, but for the next few days at least, you will have to cope with being told what to do."

Rob, Elaine, and Sharon all laughed at that. They all knew I didn't take kindly to being told what to do.

"Well, at least pass me a drink, I'm parched . . ." I muttered, my voice coming in rasps now. I'd tired myself out with my ranting, and I felt very odd as the foggy feeling returned, along with the nausea.

"Here, have a sip, just a sip mind, of my pineapple juice," Sharon said as she tilted my head forward a little and carefully placed the rim of the plastic cup against my lips. I gulped it down.

Seconds later, I regretted it. An oceanic surge of nausea hit me and without any warning I vomited the lot back onto the bed, all over me, and only missing Elaine because she'd got up to check when the nurse was coming. Seeing the mess I was in, she hurriedly hailed a passing nurse, a smiling Caribbean lady.

"Now what is all this, Barby? We told you not to drink anything straight after the anesthetic. And pineapple juice? That was the worst thing you could've had!" The nurse tutted. Elaine and Sharon almost hung their heads in shame, and both apologized profusely.

"Barby is our hero here in the ward. We've heard what she does for animals, and we feel very grateful that she's one of our patients today," the lovely nurse said in her singsong melting voice.

I smiled at that.

"Oh, Barby's a hero, alright, and we promise we'll take better care of her," said Sharon, throwing me another wink.

As the nurse worked to clean me up, I took my chance to ask her about my operation. I actually felt a bit better after being sick.

"So, how come I've got these wires coming out, and how come my bandage is so big? You're not telling me I've had keyhole surgery. I can't move my body and I feel like I've gone ten rounds with Muhammad Ali," I said, attempting a joke.

"Well, you're right, Barby," said the nurse as she wiped my face very carefully with a large moist cloth, "they had to perform a traditional surgery, cutting round the underneath of your left breast. That's why you have clips in and not just a few stitches."

"Clips?" I said, horrified. "How many?"

"There are twenty-six in there. That's why you mustn't move. You have a lot of healing to do. And the surgeons removed some lymph nodes under your armpit, so that will feel sore, too."

"They did what?" I could feel myself getting agitated again.

"Sorry, dear, that's what's written on your notes. I will ask the surgeons to speak to you on their rounds, though that'll probably be in the morning now. How's your pain, Barby?"

I grimaced. I hadn't registered the soreness when I first woke up, but now the pain was definitely building, and I could feel myself starting to panic at its intensity.

"Well, I'll bring you something for that now. Then you must settle down and let your friends take care of you. They love you, they're all here for you, now lie back and try to get better. You've had surgery, and it takes time to heal from it."

She really was the most gentle, patient nurse. Her deep brown eyes shone out of her sympathetic face.

"Yes, Nurse," I said meekly.

She returned a few moments later with a needle on a metal kidney bowl. It was the pain relief. Even though she would be inserting the tip into the cannula so it wouldn't cause any pain, I still couldn't look. Seconds later I felt a warm soothing feeling spread through my veins, and lying back suddenly seemed like an excellent thing to do.

Elaine and Sharon grinned at me.

"That's better," beamed Elaine, patting my hand and pulling out a magazine folded on the page with the crossword.

I was lucky enough to have the bed closest to the window, and as the drug progressed through my system, taking away the pain as it went, I watched the night sky draw in. The ward was quiet, only a couple of the beds in the short section were occupied, and the only sounds besides the nurses' footsteps and the flicking of magazine pages were the machines as they beeped intermittently.

"How are Harry and Ben?" I asked all of a sudden, breaking the peace and quiet that had settled on the ward.

"Oh, remembered them, have you? I thought you only had eyes for Gabby these days," Elaine sniffed. She did like to wind me up, but what she said was uncomfortably close to the truth.

"Harry and Ben are both as daft as they ever were, I expect. I'll make sure to ask Dan when we're kicked out of here. You've only been in the hospital for a day, not even a night, so I expect they're managing perfectly fine." I nodded. I loved my silly mutts, but only Gabby had stolen my heart. I know it sounds silly, but it was almost like we were the same entity split into two. Perhaps that's what people meant when they said they'd found "the one"; in doggie terms, Gabby was definitely my soul mate. I missed her terribly. The pain of being parted from her, even for just a day, felt physical. She might only be a dog, but she was the center of my increasingly frenetic and challenging world, and I needed her in order to feel whole again.

The time came for my friends to depart, and soon the ward lights were dulled and the ward went quiet again after the flurry of people leaving had died down.

I spent an uncomfortable night, not just because of the pain emanating from the place where they'd cut open my left breast, but I was also thinking about Elaine's words. She was right. I hadn't given Harry and Ben the attention they deserved and I would make it up to them on my return. I lay in the semidarkness, pondering that and the enormity of what had taken place. I prayed again that my cancer had been removed, that my Gabby wouldn't suffer without me there, and that I'd have enough love left for my other two rascal dogs when I got home.

The next morning came eventually, and the doctors began their rounds as the nurses were handing out the meds. I didn't like how woozy the painkillers made me feel, so I was happy to forgo them, despite the discomfort from the wound.

I was told that I was indeed right, that they hadn't performed keyhole surgery. I was furious, and I gave them a piece of my mind.

"Now look here," I said, trying to point my right arm, though it was difficult because of the cannula that sat on the vein running through the inside of my elbow.

"I was told I'd have a short recovery time because of it being keyhole surgery and just six stitches afterward, and I have twenty-six bleedin' clips and tubes running out of me and I'm presuming I can't go home today?"

I must have looked quite comical, with my fierce stare, my pointed finger, and all the trappings of post-surgery machinery and wires.

The consultant, whoever he was, just looked at me and blinked. "That's right, Miss Keel, we had to go in under your breast and round to the site of the tumor—there was nothing else we could do."

He then started to walk off, clipboard in hand, his colleagues already moving to the next bed.

"Now wait a minute. I'm not some old lady you can fob off! I was told six stitches . . ." I had to stop and gasp for air. The effort of being cross at these overpaid surgical gods almost finished me off.

"I'm sorry, Miss Keel. Your surgery was more complicated than we originally thought. It was necessary to cut farther along to remove the malignancy. You should be home within a week if you get some rest."

I didn't have the energy to carry on my tirade so I nodded, and sank back onto the soft pillow that was propping me up, feeling exactly like a little old lady.

Eight days later, I was finally discharged. The drain had been taken out of my body, and my wound was healing nicely. By that time I had made friends with all the nurses, and even the consultants I'd been so ready to confront. When people knew I ran the sanctuary, they were extra kind to me, treating me almost like royalty!

Wherever I go I meet people who love animals, who tell me over and over again what a wonderful job the shelter does.

It is always heartening to see the depth of feeling people have for their furry friends. All I have ever thought about is animals, yet I am always surprised when others feel the same.

I'd been told that all the cancer had gone—and that was enough for me. I didn't want to dwell on what had happened; I was too desperate to get back to the sanctuary and my beloved Gabby. The surgeons had spoken to me again about doing chemo and taking the medication, but yet again, I'd said I wouldn't consider it. I knew I risked it coming back but I also knew that I'd had enough of being messed about, albeit for my own good. I just wanted to go home.

Elaine and Rob came to get me and helped me gingerly hobble to the waiting car. I couldn't yet lift my left arm, and that whole side of me was still painful. The journey home was okay but any discomfort was easily tolerated, such was my delight at going home. Being driven into my lane, along the familiar hedgerows, past the houses that lined one side of the road, I stuck my head out of the back window and smelled the glorious scent of the English countryside: mud, grass, and the sweet heady scent of the approaching summer. It was late afternoon by the time we arrived back, and the birds were making deep-throated sounds, calling their tribe in to roost, marking their territory, just as I felt like I was marking mine by coming home.

I was home. I shuffled through the gate, Rob holding it open as wide as he could to avoid touching my small frame, afraid of accidentally hurting me, and I stepped down the small steps to my front door and once inside, I stopped for a moment. There was silence, then the clatter of paws as Harry and Ben came racing down from the living room, barking and wagging their tails furiously.

"Get down you silly dogs, oh it's good to see you, it's good to be home," I said in my soppy voice, the one I kept just for talking to my animals.

Then Gabby appeared, and she, too, ran to greet me, running around me in circles and trying to jump up.

"Gabby, my gorgeous girl," I said, delighted.

"Yap!"

I stopped dead in my tracks. Were my ears deceiving me?

"Yap!"

No, it couldn't have been Gabby, of course. But it didn't sound like Harry or Ben's low barks, either. Momentarily confused, I looked down. Gabby was wagging her tail furiously, staring up at me, her tongue hanging out. "Yap!" It was definitely her!

"She barked! She blimmin' well barked!" I shouted with glee.

Gabby looked thrilled with herself, and to prove it she yapped again.

Elaine and Rob looked at me. I looked at them, then back down at my pooch.

"Did you really do that?" I asked, feeling so overcome I was barely able to speak.

Gabby barked again in response, just to make sure we'd heard her. It was quite a high tone of a bark, but it was most definitely a proper doggie sound, the first she'd ever made.

"You barked!" I said again stupidly, stating the obvious, but it was such a joyful moment. Tears instantly sprung to my eyes, and I could feel my chin wobble. I literally had to bite back my feelings. It was the best homecoming present I could ever have had. It was the last thing this dear little creature had mastered on her journey to become a "proper" doggy. She was now a whole dog. She had healed from her wounds, and in that moment, she gave me the soaring hope that I would do the same. I felt a surge of optimism and pure love. It was an incredibly special moment, after all these months and all the work I'd put into helping her. She'd rewarded me in the best way possible.

Gabby wagged her tail even harder as if she was saying "Yes, Mummy," and started to run round my legs in circles with pure delight at seeing me, and I laughed out loud, a noise that was part sob, part cheer.

"You're a proper dog now! Oh, darling girl, I'm so proud of you."

Just then the volunteers appeared round the corner; they'd been waiting for me in the kitchen, but Gabby's barking debut had rather stolen the show. Instead of greeting me, they all started to clap Gabby for being such a clever girl.

William cheered. Diane giggled, and said, "Well done, you got there at last, eh, girl," while Dan smiled behind them.

"So, to be clear," I said, "Gabby hasn't barked while I've been away? This is genuinely the first time she's made her own yapping sound?"

"We didn't hear a peep out of her, I promise you, Barby!" grinned Di. "It really is the debut of her bark."

I could've wept with happiness. It really was a moment reserved for me by my dog. Pride and delight welled inside me.

There were others there, too. Christine had popped her head round the back door, saying, "What's all this, I thought I heard Gabby bark?" And everyone burst out laughing again.

"Now, let's get Barby into the living room and sitting down. You lot will tire her out at this rate," commanded Elaine as she took charge of the situation.

When I walked into the front room, I got the second big surprise of the day. I couldn't believe my eyes; it was filled with hundreds of cards from well-wishers and piles of presents and bunches of flowers. For once in my life, I was speechless.

"Now come this way," said Elaine again, leading me with my right arm out into the summer house on the side of my living room. Right there, sitting in between the countless stone meerkat figures, was a beautiful stone fountain with a lion's face that I'd spotted at a garden center a few months previously and had loved. I hadn't bought it, but Christine had remembered, and the staff and motley crew took up a collection while I was in hospital and had bought it for me.

A lump formed in my throat. I tried to swallow it, to say thank you, but no words came out. Instead, Gabby, tail wagging, walked up to me, plonked herself down by my legs, and barked again. She got a standing ovation for her trouble from the sanctuary staff, and seemed over the moon with the attention, which made me laugh again.

"Look at you, Gabby, look at how your confidence has grown since you arrived eight months ago. You're like a new dog," I smiled, tears forming in my eyes as I looked down at her. Her sandy-colored fur shone in the evening light and her eyes were liquid love as they stared back at me, beseechingly.

It was a perfect moment.

Chapter 15

RECOVERING

I was sitting in my sunroom, as I had done every day since my operation, in a battered black leather chair, listening to snippets of conversation among volunteers, trustees, and my staff that crackled through the walkie-talkie. These snatched moments of conversation were as fascinating to me as they were wide-ranging . . .

"Hey Christine, how's Patch in the kennels? Having any luck with training him not to jump up? He's got someone interested in him hasn't he?"

"Well, he's still got a way to go, Dan, he's a biter as well, so I really need to do lots more work on him before I can even think of rehoming him. I just wouldn't feel happy letting him go with anyone, however experienced they are with dogs, until I can bring that under control. Apart from that, he's a lovely dog—he's just never been trained."

"Well, he's in the best hands."

"Dan, would you take this folder to Di when you're en route to the pigs? Thanks."

"Alright Brenda, no problem."

"That peacock, he gets everywhere. Strutting all over the place like he owns it . . ."

"Fran, will you check on the old boy in the cattery, the one we think might have hearing problems?"

"No problem, Michael, I'm heading over there now. Are you talking about the one who had his eye removed after a car accident?"

Michael was another member of the team who had joined us recently. He had dark tousled hair and a thoughtful expression, and he'd joined us to help with the cattery and the cat rehomings, which inevitably meant he was left with lots of paperwork on his hands. He was a friendly chap and didn't seem to mind—and he'd joined the team seamlessly, fitting in to the general melee with a smile and the occasional frown over the complexities of keeping track of strays or dumped cats as well as the neutering and spaying.

It was a bright, sunny morning in June with that delicious promise of heat in the blue cloudless sky and the smell of fields and meadows as they warmed under the sunshine. Gabby was by my side, sitting at my feet, and my right hand stroked her head absentmindedly as I listened to the sound of the sanctuary coming to life that day. A cuckoo called from the nearby line of ash trees that stood in a row leading from the gate of the sanctuary up to the farm enclosure. The cockerels screeched as they paced up and down the yard, scattering the hens, who clucked in response. Fran walked past, striding out to buy milk for the morning teas with his phone on speaker. He laughed as he walked, clearly enjoying his conversation. Then there were the two dogs that barked incessantly in the kennels. I barely registered the noises, they were so normal to me.

Each day started in roughly the same way, though we never knew from one minute to the next how many animals would be left with us that day. Most volunteers and staff got to the site between dawn and 8 A.M., as animals needed feeding first thing before the business of the day began.

Usually, I would have been up with the sunrise, woken by the crowing of the roosters as they announced the new day (and every hour after that, they were so daft). Dan was usually the first up after me, and I would normally have made his staple breakfast of beans on toast before starting work. Diane would be at work from 6 A.M. most days, first heading over to the FIV cats to make sure they were all clean and had food and water. She took extra special care of them, as they were the "outsiders" of the cat world and lived separately. I think she felt sorry for them. After she'd finished there, Di would head across the yard, scattering chickens as she went, to the main cattery where her team of volunteers and coworker Fran would go about their day: cleaning out the cat pens, feeding and giving out medicine where needed, and either showing round prospective adopters or preparing those animals that had been picked for their imminent departures.

While Di was out working, I'd be answering the phones that never stop ringing, sorting out various fund-raising ideas, or gathering paperwork before heading out to help with the farm animals, accompanied by Harry, Ben, and Gabby.

Dan would be digging out areas for new pens, or helping

with fence-building, or feeding the goats, sheep, pigs, and horses. I could see them all in my mind's eye, going about their business while I sat nursing my left side, which was still sore.

One of the hardest things about my infirmity was that I couldn't pick Gabby up. I had lost count of the times I'd tried to bend over as a force of habit, before realizing my body wasn't playing ball. Gabby didn't try to jump up on me. She didn't whine to be picked up. If proof was needed that dogs instinctively sense their owners' distress or frailties, then Gabby provided it. She was considerate and sweet, sitting by me all day then snuggling next to me, but not too close so she didn't hurt me, at night.

I suddenly had time on my hands. I was too weak to work, and so I was left with my own thoughts as everyone got on with the business of the day. None of the staff had time to sit with me, there was always too much to do, and I understood this. Still, I had never spent so much time in my own company, and I couldn't help but think of my surgery and the shock of being told I had cancer. I went over and over the diagnosis in my mind, asking myself what had caused it, whether I could have prevented it, what I'd done *wrong*.

Now that the first seismic waves of disbelief had passed, I was left with an empty feeling. I really had been forced to face my own mortality. In hospital, when being wheeled to the operating theater and I'd asked God "Am I going to come out of this or not?" there was something about feeling so vulnerable, so alone in that moment, that had changed me and my attitude to life, possibly forever. There were no ready answers to any of my questions, but it didn't stop me from asking them over and over, my mind churning, my thoughts colliding then dissipating.

I had learned that I couldn't take my strength for granted any longer as I'd done throughout my life. It was a shock, another new thing to get my head around. I'd devoted my life to looking after animals without a second thought, and it was physical work, good, life-affirming, physical hard labor. I had never considered myself to have frailties; after all, I was rarely ever ill. I never caught the colds and flu that most people seemed to, and I put that down to my outdoorsy lifestyle and my determination never to let a silly thing like a cold hold me back. Being ill was for other people, or so I had thought, until now.

Up until this point in my life, I'd been busy, independent, and spirited. I'd always hated being dependent upon people and was incredibly self-reliant, even as a child. Falling ill in the way I had had knocked me sideways, though I knew myself at heart, and I knew that I would fight my way back to independence again. What I didn't know was how long it was going to take, and patience had never been my strong point.

If my volunteers confided in me, I'd always said to them, "If you've got a problem, face it, and you'll get through it." It was the one piece of advice I was grateful to my mother for. It was her motto, and even though she was a stern, unloving parent, she was as strong-minded as you could get. I needed that belligerent attitude now that I was facing my greatest battle yet.

That morning I sat and scanned that line of ash trees that were "flowering" with their distinctive bright green leaves dotted between the animal enclosures, the rabbit pens, the cattery, and the new area with a pond for the fowl, and I thought "How can you live for hundreds of years?" Those trees were so alive. The leaves shifted slightly with the soft summer breeze, but they stood so firm, so strong, so steady.

It was another question without an answer. I didn't know if I felt a sense of envy or of peace, knowing they'd be around long after I was gone.

Just then, there came a tinkling sound as Elaine popped her head round the sunroom door, and knocked one of the hundreds of wind chimes hanging from the ceiling. Gathering wind chimes was another hobby of mine. I don't know why, I just like the jangle they make when touched, the way they float above my head looking pretty. I had wind chimes of every description: metal tubes that made notes, suns orbiting planets, seahorses dancing above me, shells and glass shapes that caught the sun and refracted it into all the colors of the rainbow, and a few dream catchers for good luck. I loved each and every one of them. Everywhere my friends and volunteers went, they brought me back a pretty chime so I had ones from India, Spain, America, and many parts of the UK in a glorious cacophony of colors, shapes, and angelic sounds.

"All alright, Barby? What would you like for breakfast?" Elaine grinned, brushing aside the wind chime she'd touched with its three dolphins frolicking in the waves created from silver metal.

She knew I had the same thing every single morning: one slice of toast, baked beans, and a single slice of tomato, but it was touching that she asked me anyway. I'm a creature of habit, always have been, and I always find that cutting out decisions about the things I wasn't interested in, like food, left my mind free to think about the things that were important to me, like the animals.

"Hello, dear, it's good to see you. My usual, thank you, Elaine," I replied, trying to greet her, then wincing with the jolt of pain that suddenly appeared from along the base of my breast. The scars were still healing.

Elaine must have seen the shadow pass across my face.

"Why are you moving, m'lady? Sit there, behave yourself, madam, and I'll bring you whatever you need. Are you comfy? Do you need one of your painkillers?" she asked, looking concerned.

"No thank you, dear. I try not to take those things. I don't like taking pills, as you know," I replied, trying to smile, though the pain was momentarily intense.

"Stubborn as ever," huffed Elaine. "I've brought the paper for you, you never normally get a chance to read it . . ." Her voice trailed off as she walked away.

I chuckled at that. My friend made a joke of looking after me by pretending I was the lady of the manor. As a person, I was as far from that image as it was possible to be, and it made me laugh every time she did it.

"I can sack my staff, you know, especially if they're rude to me . . ." I countered, shouting, though the act of raising my voice always left me feeling tired. I usually had a "black belt in gob" as I liked to say, meaning I was usually the first one to make a quip or talk back to someone when I shouldn't. That had also had to change. I was like a meek little mouse these days, and I didn't like it one bit.

"Yes m'lady, anything else m'lady," laughed Elaine as she came in carrying a hot cup of tea, pretending to be my maid again.

"You can stop that right now! Put it down there, dear, where I can reach it, thank you," I smiled.

Elaine was so good to me. Every morning since I had left the hospital, she came in to make both mine and Dan's breakfasts.

"Right, now eat up. I hope you're not feeling sorry for yourself out here?" She raised an eyebrow and looked at me, knowing full well I was.

"I want to be out there, doing things . . ." I wailed. "I feel useless sitting in here, not able to help anyone or do anything. It's not like me . . ."

Elaine sighed.

"It's normal to feel like that, but you have to buck up and enjoy the rest. You haven't had many opportunities in your life to do nothing, so you might as well make the most of it. Why don't you read the paper? I'll put Gabby on your lap if you'd like, and just let everyone else make a fuss of you."

"Okay," I grumbled, looking for all the world like a child denied a lollipop.

My mood settled as my dog was placed carefully on my lap. It had been almost a year since Gabby had arrived, cowering in that car, doing her business all over the house, and utterly silent all the while. But she'd now grown in confidence far beyond my expectations. Whenever I saw this lovely girl trot outside, the dog door clattering behind her, then watching her head past my window, out to the fields, either alone or with Harry, was always a thing of beauty to me, a marvel.

I reflected on the journey we'd both undertaken, the hours spent encouraging Gabby to play with a few stuffed toys and the endless cleaning up after her. Looking after her in those first months had felt like a full-time job. I'd made a fool of myself so many times, pretending to be a dog and showing her how to pounce on a toy fox, shaking it in my mouth then springing again as fast as my then sixty-eight-year-old body could manage. I'd made myself laugh on many occasions, and I'd made my volunteers laugh as well. They all thought I was a bit bonkers anyway so I didn't care.

All my hard work had been rewarded by the peaceful, gentle dog that now lay in my lap. She was pretending to snooze, but I could see that Gabby had one ear cocked, listening to the sounds that moved around us, vibrations in the air that carried to us in that sunroom. The hens clucked contentedly now, the geese squawked and hustled for territory down by the annex, an idle bee hummed past us, settling on one of the flowerpots we had for sale under the awning in the area reserved for visitors to sit and drink their teas or eat their cake.

From the fields came Dan's voice as he joked with another volunteer, the horses neighing, and the occasional bleat from one of the lambs. I should have felt content.

I should have let the rays of sun, dappled through the trees, warm my face. I should have reveled in the novelty of doing nothing, of being looked after, of having my beloved Gabby close by me, but I just couldn't. I was too stubborn, too impatient, and the sunshine and the lazy feeling only made me feel useless. My mother always used to say that I was my own worst enemy—perhaps she was right.

I heard the bell clang at the gate. It was how visitors or suppliers alerted us to their presence. Someone must've opened it as the mailman walked past the window a few moments later and Gabby instantly perked up. She sniffed the air, registered the movement, and when he knocked on the front door, she leapt up and ran out, her tail going like the clappers of hell's bells. I couldn't help but smile at her eagerness.

The sound of her barking still filled me with joy—and I realized that Gabby had done what the sun, the care of my friends, and even the other animals couldn't do: she'd cheered me up.

Elaine answered the door. I heard her voice say "Good morning," and, a few moments after the door shut, she appeared, this time with my plate of breakfast and a small pile of envelopes.

"Open those after you've eaten, just in case they're bills," she bustled. "I've got to get going, I'm taking Rob to the doctors. Nothing to worry about," she said briskly as I opened my mouth to inquire.

And with that she was gone, leaving me to eat rather awkwardly with just my right hand and a fork, the rest of the day stretching ahead of me, knowing I'd be chair-bound until bedtime.

The bond between Gabby and I deepened in those long summer days when I sat like one of the gnomes in my garden, watching everyone come and go. I watched her with pride as she did all the things that dogs do, and when Harry came in and joined us, I felt I was being protected by my loving hounds. I'd worried that in loving Gabby so fervently, I naturally gave both Harry and Ben less of me and my emotions. I'd worried that I'd neglected them. Both Harry and Ben had been around before Gabby, and I'd always loved them, though not in the fierce way I did my newest pooch. It was hard to explain the difference, even to myself. The older dogs already had places in my heart, though, and when I saw them playing together, I knew my worries about neglecting them were groundless. Gabby was special to me, it was true, but I gave the others the same treats and cuddles, and I always felt a sense of contentment as I watched them.

Gabby was free to come and go, and yet she hovered close by me, sitting on the wooden platform that the volunteers had made for her to climb up in the sunroom so we could sit together. It was a heartfelt gesture, and I knew I was lucky to have so many good people around me. Even so, the nights were hard. I barely slept these days so I had too much time to think, to ponder upon my life. It was in the early hours of the morning that my thoughts turned to my brother Peter. Had he gone through this in his last days? Had he felt the frustration and impotence that I was experiencing?

Peter had actually been told he had leukemia but would recover. He didn't.

Of the two of us, he was always the happy-go-lucky one. He was the apple of my mother's eye—and I didn't blame her. I adored him though he was sometimes a rotter to me.

We were evacuated to Gloucester as children, and one day while we played in a field I remember vividly him saying,

"Barby"—no one except my mother ever called me Barbara—"I've made this lovely pie, do you want some?" Well, it was a cow pat so that didn't go down well. Then when we were a little older—I was ten and Peter was twelve—we joined a gang of other children and used to swing across a stream on a rope. One day, Peter said, "Shut your eyes and I'll tell you when to jump," so I did, trusting him completely. But he played another trick on me, and when I jumped I landed in the water.

"I'm drowning, I'm drowning!" I remember crying, as Peter and his pals doubled over with laughter.

"Stand up, Barby," he commanded, and I did, only to realize the stream was shallow and the water only went up to my knees. I should have realized that when I fell in, but I was panicking, and the shallow waters didn't register. I looked at Peter—his lively, lovely face alight with mischief, and I started to belly laugh, almost falling back in with the force of my happiness. I splashed him, and soon all the children had piled into the water, splashing, jumping, screeching and laughing. It was a magical time.

When my baby sister, Pam, was born that same year, it was Peter who helped me cope with my anxieties. For a start, I wouldn't let anyone else hold my baby sister. I was so possessive of her. From the moment she was born, I suffered night terrors. The bad dream was the same every time: I had taken Pam out in her perambulator, and it fell off a cliff and she fell far down to her death. I'd wake up sweating and crying out, and it was Peter who snuggled into bed beside me, whispering jokes to me in the pitch dark until I fell asleep again, groggy from fear and upset. Mother even took me to a psychiatrist to get to the bottom of those dreams, but all I remember from those sessions was being asked to do jigsaws as I presumably talked about my fears. To this day, I can pretty much do any jigsaw of any difficulty!

As I reminisced, Gabby stirred beside me. All along I had thought it was me rescuing Gabby, but in those dark nights I soon understood that it was the other way round. She soothed the memories that haunted me and the trauma of my illness. She was the epicenter of my world and the reason I got out of bed every morning. I hadn't wanted to die, not because of the sanctuary or my staff, but because I couldn't have left Gabby all alone. She was the reason I was fighting so hard to live and to regain my strength again.

She curled up in a ball of fluff beside me, keeping to my right side as if she knew that it would cause me pain to cuddle on the left. I glanced at the clock. It was 4:30 A.M., and the sky had begun to lighten. The birds were already singing the dawn chorus, and soon the rest of the animals would squawk, meow, bark, crow, bray, grunt, and cluck alongside them. Gabby stretched and yawned, sensing I was awake. A group of special needs children were arriving later in the morning. A pig needed to be rescued from a farmer's field and we needed to contact Defra. One of the cats would most likely be put down today, the old boy who was semi-blind and almost certainly deaf. I hated the thought of any animal on my site having to die, even though the poor thing had reached the end of his life span. It was all part of the circle of life that spun round every day here. Animals came in, and for others it was simply time to go. I couldn't fight it but each death left me feeling saddened. It was just another day at the Animal Sanctuary.

Chapter 16

END OF THE LINE?

"Help me lift this, will you, dear?" I shouted to Christine, who was passing. It was a hot morning in July, and I was starting to take little trips outside, beyond the perimeters of my bungalow, though my energy levels were still appallingly low.

Smiling, she came over to me, a piece of grass clinging to her blonde pigtails as she walked. She was wearing a jade-colored T-shirt over a pair of disheveled jeans and wellies. She looked like a woman in her element—that of the earth, nature, and sunshine. I blinked as I watched her against the sunlight, catching a streak of black and white out of the corner of my eye.

It was Dee, Christine's faithful collie. Wherever Christine was, her dog was never far behind, her nose to the ground, investigating each scent on every fence post, every blade of grass. She was so clearly a worker dog, always on alert, always moving everywhere with a kind of intense focus.

For a moment I compared her to my Gabby—the pair

179

couldn't have been more different. Where Gabby was soft and pliable, Dee was focused and alert. Where Gabby was undemanding of attention or walks, Dee needed lots of exercise, and lots of stimulation. Collies are clever dogs. They go a bit mad if they're bored, and so Christine walked for miles each day with her, and she was even used to rounding up some of our wayward sheep on the odd occasion they got through the hedgerows surrounding their field. Gabby was content to sit beside me for hours while I convalesced, but Dee would have ripped the sunroom down if she'd have been expected to stay in there for a whole day. Such different personalities in the same species.

Christine had moved into the caravan on-site, which sat close to the kennels so she could be available to take in strays or abandoned dogs that were dumped or brought in overnight. She was devoted to dogs and was always calm and friendly to everyone around the site. She didn't get involved in the day-to-day politics that seemed an inevitable part of working in a team; she rose above all the quarrels, all the fallings-out, and managed, somehow, to stay in everybody's good books. She was as close to a saint as you could get in bodily form, or that's what I used to tell her. In response, she'd look momentarily puzzled, then she'd smile, her sweet features accepting the compliment without a hint of arrogance. She was always useful, always on hand, and yet she never shared her troubles or concerns. She was a private person, extremely self-reliant, and I respected her enormously.

"I'm right here, Barby. Now what are you trying to do? Should you be attempting to lift the goat mix?" She stood with both hands on her hips, legs slightly apart, and frowned at me, though a smile played on her lips.

I had to laugh.

"No, of course I'm not supposed to lift anything heavy yet, but I need to do *something*, otherwise I'll go completely crazy." Christine looked at me for a moment, registering my need to help without telling me off or dismissing me like a child.

"Okay, why don't you come to the kennels and help feed the dogs while I shift this for you? I'll meet you back here in ten minutes and we can feed the goats together."

That's what I liked about Christine. She was always practical. She never got cross or upset, preferring instead to find a solution.

I made my way slowly down from the farm animal enclosures to the kennels on the south side of the sanctuary, passing a group of volunteers huddled round having a chinwag.

"Alright, Barby, how are you?" asked one.

I waved and smiled. "I'm fine, thank you, dear," but I didn't stop to join in their chat.

The truth was I wasn't feeling fine at all. I knew that I wouldn't make it down to the kennels, I'd have to go back to my chair as I felt on the verge of collapse with exhaustion.

Gabby, my little shadow, was, as ever, by my side. We diverted in through the front door and I flopped into my chair, sighing with relief tinged with sadness. I fully admit I am an obstinate, strong-willed woman, and this enforced rest filled me with frustration and resentment. I even think I let out an "urghhhhhhh" sound, which made Gabby's ears twitch backward.

"It's okay, girl, I'm just feeling nettled today. I'm not using that bloody wheelchair, either. I'll wait till I'm well enough to walk again."

The wheelchair was the bane of my life. Diane insisted I use it so I could be pushed around the site, but I hated the sight of it. It was one of our stock of sanctuary chairs that we kept to help our disabled or elderly visitors navigate the site, so it was a bit scruffy and smelled of mildew as it was kept in the sheds over the winter. It wasn't the condition of it that bothered me—it was the fact that I had to use it at all.

Christine had been sensitive in not mentioning it, or perhaps she knew from experience that she'd have caught a piece of my mind if she had.

I knew I was weak. I still felt pain, even though the wound under my breast had healed nicely. I was still cross with the surgeons, feeling that my body had been "mucked about" with, and there were plenty of times I regretted even going for that original scan. In some ways I wished I'd never opened that envelope and had carried on as usual.

The past is impossible to change, and just as I'd seen with Gabby, some things, once set in motion, had to run their own course—in their own time.

Would I have just carried on, feeling healthy and well? I didn't know the answer, but there were times I thought to myself privately that if only Christine hadn't been so insistent about me going to my mammogram, I wouldn't have ended up feeling as helpless and dependent as I did right now. I never said that to her. I valued her wisdom and friendship too much, but, looking back, I think part of me blamed her for my current predicament, however unfair that was.

Gabby looked up at me, sheer bemusement written on her face. She looked particularly pretty today with the black fur around her eyes, looking for all the world like she had ringed them with kohl. In certain lights, her eyes appeared almost amber-colored. They lost their darkness, and today I could see flecks of gold in them. She muzzled her white nose into my hand and I felt the cold wet shock of her nose as she sniffed then licked me. Her ears dropped down with straggly honey fur either side of them, which made her look adoringly bedraggled.

"Don't worry, girl, I haven't lost my marbles . . . yet. Now where are those raffle tickets? I'd better get back to sorting them."

Our annual Open Day was coming up in a few short weeks, and the staff were all frantically preparing the site for the influx of people that usually swamped us on the day. As we relied on the event to provide a good proportion of our income for the year, it was all hands on deck in the run-up to this important day, with raffles, vendor booths, events and, of course, the animals on show. The whole site needed to be thoroughly cleaned. The tearooms and the seating areas needed to be cleared and restocked. The animal pens needed to be checked, reinforced if needed, or fixed. I needed to publicize the event, which meant a call to the *Bexhill Observer* and other smaller local publications, and I needed to make sure we had our paperwork up to date for anyone who wanted to sponsor an animal or become a member of the sanctuary for a small annual fee.

Last year I was running about, bossing everyone around, making decisions, and chatting to our visitors. This year, in sharp contrast, I was confined to my chair or the wheelchair. It was clear to me that I was not physically strong enough to help with the animals by lifting bales of hay or dragging large sacks of feed like I normally would.

I had never before felt useless, but now I did, and it wasn't a pleasant feeling. Diane had suggested I take on small jobs that needed doing but that there never seemed enough time for, like tearing out the raffle tickets in advance of the drawing, writing out signs and notices, filling out paperwork, and doing admin jobs. I could have screamed with frustration. I had always found administrative work dull compared to being outside doing what I loved best, though I recognized that a certain amount of paper-pushing was necessary in running a sanctuary. But now it was all I could do, and frustration mounted as I tore apart each ticket with more gusto than was perhaps called for.

With each passing day, my vexation grew. I liked being in the thick of things, and the Open Day was always our chance, as a shelter, to shine. It was my favorite event of the year, even more so than the Christmas Bazaar and the many raffles and bring-and-buy sales we held throughout the year, and I was desperate to be out in the fields helping the others make everything ready.

Christine came and found me. The chimes trickled sound

through the room as she walked, wafting her hand through the metal hangings as quietly as a breeze.

"You look very sorry for yourself," was all she said.

I nodded in reply, suddenly feeling tears well up. I wiped them away, hoping she hadn't seen them.

"What's the news around the place, then?" I said, in part to divert attention away from my emotional state.

Christine had such a warm, loving spirit. She gave me a look of understanding. She leaned over and touched my hand lightly.

"Oh, the usual. It's very busy down in the field, but I've spoken to Diane, and when you've had a rest, she will wheel you down there so you can be there and keep an eye on everything. You know you can't walk down there. It tires you out too much . . ." Christine's voice was soft, but I felt the steel underneath it.

I nodded.

"Gabby and me will be there, in that blinkin' chair." Suddenly there was a hullabaloo outside.

"What's all that noise?" I said, startled.

Christine stood up and peered over at the gate, which was visible at the end of the yard.

"The gate's open. I think it's Fran bringing in the horses. . . . Yes, there's the horse box going through. Oh gosh, I can hear them kicking the side of the van. I'd better go and see if I can help."

Christine dashed out, the chimes jangling with the hurry of her departure. I turned my leather chair round on its wheel, and watched her go, feeling forlorn.

A member of the public had called in to the sanctuary to report two horses that weren't being fed. They lived on the far outer reaches of a farm in Sussex, and the farmer appeared to have either forgotten about them or simply didn't want them anymore. The person who rang in, a young-sounding man, said he'd been feeding them, and had reported it to a larger animal charity. The charity had put a notice on the fence of the field the horses lived in, asking for the owner to contact them. As far as he knew, no one had done so, as the horses still weren't being given any food, apart from what this man was providing.

Once Fran got wind of this, he shot down to the farm and talked to the owner, who reluctantly agreed to give us the horses, which were half wild, having been abandoned in their field, left to themselves for goodness knows how long. It was Fran's job to bridle them today and transport them back to the shelter—not the easiest task, and he'd left here at the crack of dawn to rein them in. I could hear them whinnying, and the crack of their shoes against the inside of the box and I didn't envy Fran his task one bit.

A couple of hours later, Fran marched past my sunroom into the sitting room.

"How was it, dear?" I asked, seeing that his face was cut and bleeding.

"It took ages to get the head collars and bridles on them. There's a roan, she's a lovely brown nut color with a white stripe up her face, and the other one's a dun, he's got the black stripe down his back and the stripes on his forelegs. They're wild—they were rearing up, trying to kick my head."

Fran wasn't a small man. He had a sturdy build, strong enough to be one of those who brought in the wilder large animals, yet he was incredibly tender toward them. He wore a ripped T-shirt, which must've got damaged during the tussle, faded jeans that had seen better days, and mud-encrusted heavy boots. He would've needed them. I have always had an innate fear of horses. They're the only animal I won't deal with personally. I don't mind keeping them and caring for them, of course, but I won't handle them, for exactly that reason; they frighten me when they rear up. The two horses appeared to have had the opposite effect on Fran—he seemed energized by the struggle.

"I'm going to go and see how they're doing. We've put them in the field behind your garden, to the right. They've got a decent-sized paddock there and shelter for the winter."

"Alright, dear, you take care of yourself," I added as he left.

"Come up here, Gabby, can you climb up?" I whispered, patting my lap with my right hand.

Something about those horses, and how they'd been brought to heel, made me shudder. It felt uncomfortably like the way I was feeling now: trapped, subdued, angry. Even though it was all obviously for the horses' benefit, I still saw a parallel between them and me. I felt bridled by my illness. I felt wild anger at my "imprisonment," just as they did.

I needed a cuddle with Gabby. On the third attempt, Gabby managed to climb onto my legs, and she sat upright, her tail gently wagging, and licked my nose.

"Are you kissing me? Do you want a kiss, lovely girl?" I

crooned to her as if she was a baby. Gabby loved the attention. Her dear little face cocked to one side as if she was trying to understand me, reflecting my face, as I petted her.

Despite the fact that Diane came in, as promised, and wheeled me down to the end field where the bulk of the Open Day events were taking place, I still felt cross.

I guessed I'd succumbed to a bout of self-pity, which I wasn't proud of, and I tried to bat away my feelings like I would an annoying fly. Despite the sunshine, the busyness of all the volunteers setting up booths, hanging bunting, and arranging chairs and tables, I felt a black cloud hover nearby, even though it had been almost three months since the operation.

"Barby, should I put this here?" one young volunteer asked me.

"That's fine, dear, put it where you like," I replied.

"Where do you want these chairs, Barby?" called another.

"They're fine there. Yes, just there. No, don't put them behind the table, or we won't be able to sit on them. Goodness me," I replied with more than a hint of exasperation.

"Do you want the raffle at the usual time?" asked someone else. I felt irritation bubble up again, but I managed to put a smile on my face and replied, "Yes, please, dear, thank you."

I'd been standing up at one of the tables helping to pin up signs when I suddenly felt all my energy leave me. Gabby placed one paw on my leg, and I looked down at her. Her face seemed to have a quizzical expression. She blinked, and her dark eyelashes stole the expression away. Perhaps it had been my imagination. Perhaps Gabby didn't understand how I felt, but I knew, deep down, she did. She was telling me to stop.

"Okay, Gabby, I'm going back now to have a lie-down. Why don't you hop on and we can be pushed together?"

By the time Di had trundled us back up to the bungalow, I felt faint with exhaustion.

"I'm just going for a nap," I said to Di. "I don't need anything. You go and make yourself busy. There's so much to do, I don't know how we'll manage it in time . . ." My voice trailed off, and Di, recognizing I was getting beyond comprehension, helped me out of the chair and quietly shut my bedroom door. Troubling thoughts had begun to cluster in my mind. Was I able to carry on running the sanctuary? And most upsetting of all, did I want to continue?

Gabby curled into a ball next to me on the bed. Harry and Ben settled on the floor, and I lay back, drifting into a dreamless sleep.

The next morning I was woken by the roosters, the first one letting rip just after 4 A.M. This set the others off. One by one, around the arc of the sanctuary, each rooster started to crow, like a domino effect.

"Bloody birds," I said to myself, which made Gabby's ears prick up. "There's no use you waking up now, it's far too early," I said, ruffling the dog's fur, and at that moment, as Gabby sank back down onto the blankets, I realized I didn't want to get up.

I'd never had that feeling in my life. I was always first up, ready for whatever the day would bring, my only thoughts being for the creatures that lived on my land.

Today was different. I didn't want to sit in the sunroom listening to the vivid life of the sanctuary. I didn't want to be wheeled about everywhere, but worst of all, I didn't want to join in with the work or the people, either. I felt that the whole world could go to hell and I wouldn't care a jot. I felt a black hole open up in my chest, a sadness that felt heavy, lying over me like a thick blanket. This wasn't me. I was cross, yes. Irritable, definitely! But melancholy, never. I had never not wanted to feed the animals or stroke the pigs in the dawn light. I had never not wanted to call to the cats as they prowled in their large pens, telling them to stop their mewling. I had never once not wanted to break bread for the birds or shout for Peter the Peacock. This strange new emotion stifled me and left me feeling numb.

My whole existence had been wrapped up in the sanctuary for so long that doing anything else was unthinkable, and yet I had started to question it. Perhaps it was delayed shock from the illness. Perhaps it was a kind of depression, one that so many people experience after suffering from cancer. Or perhaps I was simply too tired to go on with my life as it was, and I needed to feel there was another way for me. I didn't know. I just knew that I was thinking the time had come to leave the shelter, to withdraw and find some peace somewhere, and that feeling terrified me.

Should I give up the sanctuary? Should I retire at last and settle somewhere else with just Gabby, Harry, and Ben? Should I turn my back on everything I knew? Was it the end for the Animal Sanctuary?

I didn't know. I lay there for a moment before making a decision to get up and go for a walk. My health wasn't really up to it. My recovery had been slow since the surgery, and most of the time I had pottered around the yard and the cattery rather than striding off anywhere more adventurous. I was fed up, though, with how small my world had become. It was time to push the boundaries again, if I was ever going to recover fully. I needed to clear my head before the volunteers arrived to start work. I couldn't speak to anybody with my mind fractured like this.

Slowly, I eased myself out of the covers, whispering to Gabby as I went. I was wearing a clean T-shirt, so I decided to pull on a pair of sweatpants and head out as I was. The animals didn't care whether I'd brushed my hair.

We walked slowly and in silence, surrounded by lush countryside, past the elder tree next to the annex, past the hawthorn tree, down through the farm enclosure to the back fields. I stopped for a moment when I came to Brian's tree—a horse chestnut that was settling in nicely. Standing there, I couldn't help but ponder the fragility of life, and how we were all here on this planet by the grace of God. I stroked the bark and said a quiet prayer, thanking Brian for his gift to us and hoping he was resting in peace at last. When I'd finished murmuring, I carried on and didn't stop until we came to the end of the bottom field. Here I could see fields and acres of grassland in a 180-degree vista around me. I knew I was pushing it regarding my physical strength, but today I felt it was worth the exertion. I had to stop, I was so out of breath. Even in the few weeks of recuperation, my fitness had plummeted. I sat down on one of the tree stumps, Gabby sniffed around my legs then chose the exact clump of grass she would wee against. As Gabby cocked her leg, she looked over at me, her eyes doleful and adoring, and I couldn't help but smile.

When we had started the walk, the light had been dim but increasing, and now the sky was beginning to arch over us with that intense blue of summer. I breathed in, taking in a lungful of the fresh morning air. Dew still trembled on the blades of grass. An ant walked past carrying a yellow green leaf, and I felt my heart lift at the sight of it.

How could I leave this place? My body and soul were intertwined with every plant, every tree, every creature that walked on four legs here. Behind me the goats were cropping the grass, ignoring me as I shared their space, soaking in the soft rising sunlight.

"I have to stay, Gabby, this is my home, and yours." She walked over to me and yawned, settling herself down at my ankles.

"Whatever comes next, I have to face it. I would never abandon these animals who have already been left. I couldn't do it. No, I have to face this. I have to go ahead with the Open Day, and not just because it is getting too late to cancel, because it's that or leave the sanctuary completely."

Gabby looked up at me.

"Let's go, girl, we've got work to do," I said, rising back up, and starting the slow process of walking back up to the house where the business of the day would soon begin.

Chapter 17

THE SADNESS LIFTS

"Barby, get to the front gate as quick as you can."

Di's voice crackled over the walkie-talkie. It was seven o'clock, and I was out giving my dogs their morning walk. The air felt cool against my skin, and the early dew soaked the dogs' paws. The birds scattered as they saw us coming. The two rescued horses sniffed in our direction, watching us as we traced our way round the back field and up to my garden. Cautiously, the roan approached.

"I've got no food for you yet," I called to her, not wanting to get too close. Gabby, sensing my disquiet around horses, stayed close to my ankles, while Harry and Ben lolloped over to them, wagging their tails, causing the mare to back off, wafting her thick tail at us in disgust.

I pressed the side button and spoke back, my face creased in a frown. "Why, what's happening?"

"Just get here, quickly," Di said and buzzed off.

Puzzled, I hobbled toward the house, all three dogs following me.

"Go inside, I don't know what's happening," I said to them, forever protective of my mutts. It never for a moment crossed my mind that perhaps they should protect me.

I shut the chain-link fence behind me to stop the dogs getting through, and left all three of them staring at me in a line as I walked as fast as I could to the main entrance.

I saw instantly we had trouble. A woman with a pinched face was squaring up to Diane. She held a large black trash can in her arms. The gate was open, but the woman was standing on the boundary as if she was scared—or reluctant—to come inside.

"This person is dumping these cats here," Di said, her voice high with indignation. She looked flustered. Her hair had escaped from the scrunchie she used to tie it back, giving her a rather disheveled appearance, and her face was red.

"What cats? I can't see any," I said, looking round.

The woman standing outside the gate was youngish with scraped-back hair. I looked over at her, but she wouldn't catch my eye. She was holding out that black trash can, offering it to Diane. I turned to my colleague, a look of "What's all this?" on my face.

Di looked at it pointedly.

"The cat's in there?" I exploded, suddenly realizing what all this was about.

I looked the woman full in the face but she would not meet my gaze.

"There's another in the basket in my car. I've got to go, my baby's in there."

She ran to the car, pulled out a wicker basket, from the bottom of which came a pathetic mewling noise.

By now I was holding the trash can in my arms. I felt something move inside. Horrified, I opened the swing lid and saw a black shape at the bottom, shaking with fear.

"You wouldn't put your bleedin' baby in a trash can, so why a cat?" I yelled, not caring who heard me.

"Now, calm down, Barby. Don't upset yourself, you've been ill, don't forget." Di tried to warn me, but it was too late. All my angers and fears, all the emotion that had been bottled up inside me since my diagnosis now flowed out in a great torrent of disbelief and rage.

"It's the middle of the summer, and you've put a cat in a black trash can. You could've suffocated it. You could've killed it!" The woman looked harassed, and Di stepped in front of me.

"I'll take the basket. Now go to the cattery, Barby, and I'll join you there," she said in her usual measured voice, but I wouldn't budge.

"Not on your nelly! I'm not going until she's left," I shouted.

By now, the woman had handed the wicker container to Di, and she threw herself back into her car as quickly as she could, and I heard her clutch squeal as she tried to reverse her car in a hurry.

"Serve her right if her clutch dies," I muttered under my breath.

When it came to animal cruelty I was unbending in my

convictions, though I didn't normally show my feelings like this. I had become ultrasensitive because of the illness, so I just let rip, although I wasn't proud of myself afterward.

"Get yourself—and more importantly the cat—to the cattery," Di said. "We need to see if it's okay. Being bumped about in that awful trash can will have upset the poor thing. It'll be frightened and possibly hurt."

I nodded. What Di said made perfect sense, but I wanted to know that woman had left my land. I was fuming, furious, and again I refused to move an inch.

When the woman had finally driven out, turning into the lane without looking, or so it seemed, I carried the trash can to the squat building, my newly aroused anger and indignation giving me newfound strength. I walked along the path of paving stones and gravel, past the mewing cats, their tails aloft, curling around the posts inside their pens, carrying my charge.

Inside, we placed the animals carefully on the table. Di opened the trash can and carefully lifted the cat out, trying not to get scratched or bitten in the process. It was a small black-and-white cat, and it looked to be in surprisingly good shape considering the means of transportation it had endured.

The other cat lay in the basket and was more reluctant to come out. It too was black and white.

"They're probably brother and sister," Di said conversationally, "and they both look okay. The things some people do . . ." she added as she inspected both cats.

"Go and have a rest, you look done in," she implored, one

eyebrow raised in that way of hers. "They're both safe now. I can look after them from here."

I recognized that look and knew she'd brook no argument.

I walked away, feeling the anger start to drain from my body, leaving behind a sense of complete exhaustion.

Later that night, sleep eluded me. The day had been a difficult one all round. I still couldn't wrap my head around how someone could put a cat in a bin. It seemed unthinkable—and yet it wasn't my job to judge, however fierce I was, however *right* I was. Perhaps that woman had intolerable pressures on her. Perhaps she didn't have the money for cat baskets. Perhaps she was a single mum, facing eviction from her apartment, or feeling overwhelmed by a baby and animals. Who knew? One thing was positive: she hadn't dumped them, and instead she'd brought them to safety.

At least the pain under my arm was receding as each day passed. I lay there, stroking Gabby as she snuffled beside me, always happy to just sit with me, to stay with me through thick and thin. Suddenly I felt fortunate. I was happy with my lot, really. I'd just been knocked sideways by the surgery, but it didn't mean I wouldn't recover, that I wouldn't be stronger and fitter as a result.

I looked down at my fluffy, honey-colored dog and kissed her head softly.

"We're survivors, you and me. We've both been through so much, and yet here we are, living another day."

I realized it was time to throw myself back in to living my life again. This time without any regrets, without any doubts.

Chapter 18

A ROLLER-COASTER RIDE

Every one of my helpers is a gem, I mused to myself as I watched William stride to the field with a shovel, Dan tip a load of old boxes and crates into a temporary skip, and Fran saunter back up toward the house with the morning's milk supply, even though he was a staunch vegan. They all had their special jobs to do. They all just came in and got on with it.

I think that's the secret of our success, I thought, as activity buzzed all around me. *They all pull together and appreciate what the sanctuary does for the many animals here.*

Over the past year we'd had, on average, seven new animals arriving each day, and after a rough count, we now had approximately five hundred creatures being loved back to health and happiness on the site.

In that moment, a bright August morning, I felt very honored to have such a committed, passionate team.

Christine walked past, an English bull terrier called Juke straining at the leash, taking him for a walk before she started arranging the hanging baskets that she created so beautifully for the Open Day each year to decorate the site for the enjoyment of visitors, but also a few extra to sell. Di hurried down to the booths with the box of raffle tickets for our grand prize drawing later in the afternoon. Visitors would be arriving at 2 P.M., but there was still plenty to do to get ready, the finishing touches still needed to be made.

Whatever crisis popped up, and they seemed to happen on a daily basis, my team was behind me, helping each other, working so hard to keep the sanctuary and the shop going. The sanctuary was in good heart, and as the sun warmed my face, I felt a sense of contentment around the site, a welcome communal happiness that had infected everyone now that the big day had arrived.

The sanctuary charity had purchased an adjacent plot of land, which we had sorely needed due to the increase in our animal numbers, so things were definitely improving. It was an amazing feeling to stand at my sink each morning and look out of the kitchen window, knowing the land almost as far as I could see was now owned by the shelter. Already, the goats had been moved farther down into the new land to make room for a larger paddock for the ponies and give more space to the horses.

The line of trees at the edge of my vision marked the boundary of the expanded land. It gave me a feeling of solidity and strength as I took in the view, a sense that one day I would leave behind a legacy. It could be a harsh world out there, both for animals and humans. What I had created out of such humble beginnings was a place where people and creatures could feel safe, a place where they could belong. Many times, visitors had told me that when they walked through the sanctuary gates they felt an overwhelming feeling of love within the walls and fences, the tree-lined fields and enclosures, and I couldn't deny it. I only hoped that one day, places like this would not be necessary because owners would treat their charges with the care and love they deserved. That day hadn't arrived, and until then, we did everything we could, day after day, to pick up the pieces for the animals who were given to us.

Outside, the trees were in full green regalia, and gave shade and shelter whatever the weather. The usual animal sounds surrounded me but I barely noticed them; I was so used to the crowing, clucking, screeching, barking, meowing, quacking, and neighing that permeated every inch of our environment.

"Thinking again, are we, Barby? You're getting very reflective in your old age." It was Di, who had walked in to find me.

Even though I was well enough to walk down to the field, my friend had insisted that today I was to be pushed down in that bloody wheelchair. I knew she was worried that I'd tire myself out too much helping get things ready and I'd have no energy left for the actual event later on. She was probably right, but I would never have admitted it. Since my surgery, she liked to mollycoddle me, which drove me mad, but I knew her concern came from kindness, and so I didn't dare utter a word, nodding my head in agreement.

"I can't help myself these days," I sighed.

Already I felt the edge of irritable exhaustion prickle at me, waiting to strike if anyone said the wrong thing to me.

"Well, you can stop thinking, and stop sighing, because I'm here to take you down to the field. No complaints necessary!"

I had to laugh at that.

For once, I didn't mind letting her take charge. It was nice to feel looked after, I suddenly realized, though I was desperate to reclaim my health and fitness in full. Thank goodness she'd never cottoned on to the fact I took a morning walk with Gabby every day now. She'd have blasted me for doing that, probably rightly, because if I fell or was ill I could be in the field for hours before anyone found me. I'd been fine, though, and gradually I felt my health returning, though it was painfully slow.

"And don't think I don't know about your walks with Gabby every morning. I'm awake as soon as the first rooster starts crowing, or did you forget? I see you walk past my window every day." She grinned, waiting for me to follow her outside.

"You scoundrel," I pouted, "why didn't you say anything? Here I was, thinking I was having some quiet *private* time." (I put great emphasis on that word to make my point.)

"Come on, Gabby, there's a good girl, we've been rumbled, found out . . ."

I muttered as I walked, though still at a slow pace. Gabby appeared by my ankles as if by magic. She was never far away. The little dog scrambled up onto my lap as Di pushed us both down in my wheelchair. I maintained as regal a pose as I could, but by the time we reached where the booths had been set up, I was more like a worker bee scanning each and every one, making a mental list of what needing doing.

"Thank you, Diane, though it wasn't necessary," I said. I couldn't resist a dig at her. I'm such a wicked old witch.

"Blast it, I've forgotten the eggs. Diane, dear, would you go back and fetch them? They're by the sink in the kitchen. Thank you, dearest."

Diane didn't answer, except to salute me, smile, and walk back the way we'd come. I watched her go for a moment, grateful for her selfless work.

Rows and rows of freshly cleaned eggs were sitting waiting in a series of large egg boxes inside. I'd been up at dawn scrubbing each of them as hard as I dared. We often found that people bought more eggs if they were clean rather than straight from the chicken's roost with tufts of straw and bird poo on them. The job of cleaning them now fell to me as it was something I could do sitting down in the house.

Earlier in the year, I'd also planted five hundred seedlings, ready to be nurtured and sold today. Several tables had been put aside to display the assorted flowers in their pots, and I looked at them with satisfaction, seeing a job well done.

Next to that booth were some of Christine's hanging baskets. She was busy arranging them and putting prices on some of them to sell later on.

"They look good, Christine," I exclaimed, pleased to see how pretty the pinks and reds of the geraniums looked. I wanted the booth next to that one to be where the raffle prizes were displayed. I'd spent many months calling local businesses asking them to donate hampers, gardening supplies, days out, bottles of wine, or toys and games for the awards, and I'd been rewarded with a mountain of prizes, so many that we needed two tables to hold them on. We had also started to make gifts ourselves for sale. I'd asked Harry, another of my recently joined volunteers who knew his way round a lathe and saw, to cut me pieces of wood in the shape of cats, which I then made into magazine or letter stands. Part of my recovery time had been spent painting those cats, creating a series of black-and-white, ginger, or tabby cats, and my instinct was that they would sell like hotcakes.

I stopped for a brief moment to admire my handiwork. I'd always enjoyed painting—I am a practical person, and I like being creative, so this was a way of helping me overcome the boredom and feelings of uselessness at my current condition.

As I took charge, Gabby took the chance to sniff at the earth and plants. It must have been heaven for her, being surrounded by delicious smells and so many people who stopped to fuss over her or stroke her. She was definitely a very popular dog. I beamed at her with pride.

At that moment, William walked past with a stack of chairs.

"No, dear, you'll have to put the chairs over there, we're reserving this area for the raffle prizes being handed out," I called to him.

"Over here then?" he asked. He looked hot, his face pink with exertion as he worked.

"That's right, thank you, William. Now would you mind helping me sort through these raffle prizes? Some of them haven't got numbers on, so they need one."

Walking over to me, Christine said, "I shall be glad when everyone has spent their money, eaten the cake, drunk their tea, and gone home."

It was most unlike her.

"Anything wrong, Christine? It's not like you to be a pessimist. You've been working here too long!"

"Sorry, Barby, I just had to say good-bye to Tilly, one of the terriers we rehomed. She was a sweet little thing, and I'd grown to enjoy our walks together." Christine smiled, but I could see the pain of missing that little dog all over her face.

"Why don't you go and get us both a nice cup of tea? It's tough for all of us when an animal we've grown to care for is rehomed. I'm sorry you feel sad, dearest," I said as kindly as I could.

We were all here because we cared so devotedly for the animals, and it was often an emotional roller coaster as we took them on a journey from abandonment through to good health and happiness, and, of course, rehoming if we could. Each animal left its mark on us, for better or for worse, and often we got more emotionally involved than we should. Every day brought new highs—and frequent lows—yet we had to remain focused on the good we were doing, the love we were giving to these animals, and the huge amount of help we needed to keep going. Running a sanctuary wasn't for the fainthearted, and I was incredibly proud of every single person who gave their time and compassion to the charity.

"I know, I know. I'll just miss her, that's all," Christine said. "Do you want sugar?"

"Yes please, four sugars," I smiled, "with just a dash of milk, that's all."

There was no point in trying to talk Christine out of her feelings. We all became overly attached to the animals; I was proof of that with Gabby, and it was hard seeing them go, though we also celebrated each dog's new lease on life in a happy, permanent home.

The beginning of the month had been wet, and we'd wondered if the bazaar would take place at all. We usually pressed ahead anyway, but the risk was that fewer people would come and we'd raise significantly less money. It was amazing how much difference the weather made to our income. Luckily, the sun had come out this morning, and fingers crossed, we would have a good turnout.

Christine returned with two mugs of tea. We sat on the nearby chairs, which had been set up for visitors. Dee and Gabby played together for a while, lazily rolling on the grass as the sky arched blue over our heads and the heat of the day settled upon us.

"The hordes will be here any minute, it's nearly midday . . ." she said, batting off a particularly persistent fly. We ran a free minibus service from Bexhill town center for people who wouldn't otherwise be able to get here—and the first drop-off was due any second.

"Let's just enjoy this while we can, it's going to be a busy day," I said, closing my eyes and feeling the warmth of the sun on my face. It was a pleasant feeling. People shouted or called instructions around us. Gabby yawned, and a wasp buzzed past, on its way to the cake booth, no doubt.

In those relaxing few moments before our visitors arrived, I realized that I wasn't just a figurehead for the sanctuary, I was vital to the sanctuary. It was me everyone turned to in order to lead the charity, to hand out advice or take charge of things when needed. It was me who people recognized, who gave so willingly of their time and even money for the animals' cause. That was because my name was now synonymous with animal welfare in the Bexhill area. It was me who oversaw the setting up of the booths today, who created the competitions and gathered in the prizes; it was me who oversaw the structural development of the site, the new fences, new buildings, and how different legacies and donations were handled. It was me who answered the phones, giving a listening ear to those who needed to give up beloved pets or dump unwanted creatures. Either way, I was there for anyone who needed me. And I would be nothing without the hard work of everyone around me, and especially the trustees of the charity who worked so tirelessly, without pay or recognition, to forward the cause of so many animals who needed our care.

I had vowed when I started the Animal Sanctuary that no animal would be put down, unless it would otherwise suffer. That policy meant we were always full to bursting, always having to fund-raise to cover the vets' bills every month, and always looking for new ways to expand our work and help as many fellow beasts as possible. It was an astonishing achievement, I saw that now, and it had taken me a lifetime to get to this point. I think in all the weeks of self-doubt and depression since my cancer diagnosis, I'd allowed myself to forget that the sanctuary needed me. Whereas I'd spent my life feeling useful and busy, I'd suddenly felt useless and ill, and I hadn't liked it one bit. I'd worried my physical stamina wouldn't return, that I would therefore be pointless to every-one and everything here.

As I sat sipping my drink, I saw things rather differently. I realized I couldn't give this up, because what would happen if I did? If I walked away and retired, who would run it, who would be in charge? I don't think any of the volunteers, staff, or trustees would willingly take all this on. It was a twenty-four-hour occupation. Running the sanctuary wasn't just a job, it was a way of life, and I honestly couldn't think of any-one who would give up their freedom, their lives or their re-laxation to take all this on. And I wouldn't expect them to. It was too much for me, really, I also knew that because of this illness, and perhaps also because of my advancing years. Yet, it was my life—and every single animal that came through my front gate was welcome to live here with me or be rehomed into loving families. What a gift that life was. What a privi-lege.

I finished my drink, putting my cup down to balance rather awkwardly against a clump of grass. The first trickle of people appeared at the gate, and Christine was already up and waving them to come in and make themselves at home. I gazed around, marveling at the sight of so much love in one place, then putting on my welcoming face, I stood up. It was time to enjoy myself, to become the Barby Keel that everyone wanted to see, and to raise as much money as possible for the charity.

Gabby was instantly back by my side, and as I started min-gling and saying hello to old friends who supported us every year, she was ready to walk with me. My faithful dog. Always with me. Always by my side. She had repaid my kindness a million times over.

"Darling girl, it was you who rescued me," I whispered and Gabby's ears pricked up as I spoke. Then I turned to greet a visitor and our special annual event unfolded through that sunny afternoon.

EPILOGUE

The Summer Bazaar was a roaring success. It raised thousands of pounds for the sanctuary, enough to keep us afloat through the coming winter. There was a palpable sense of achievement from the volunteers afterward, as they'd seen people flock to support the animals because of all their hard work. It was a golden moment in time, a rare point where I could breathe and feel that I'd finally shaken off my troubles, and those of the constant demands of the site, even for just a few months.

Just then there was a bark, and Harry and Ben loped over to me as I fed one of the pigs a loaf of bread at the back of my garden They'd run off and circled the land during our walk, and they returned with gusto: tails wagging, tongues lolling out of their mouths as they panted with exertion. Three fine, handsome dogs. I was a proud owner indeed that morning. Gabby rolled in the grass with the retriever and the spaniel and, as I grinned over at them, I reflected again that whatever help I'd given my funny Yorkie cross, she'd repaid me a million times over. The last few months had been bleak. There was no denying it—she had gotten me through all of it. I'd faced my own demons and come out the other side.

She was now a fully formed "proper" dog. She could play, bark, and go outside to go to the toilet. She played with abandon; there was no hint of the cowering beast that had turned up that fateful day. As if in answer to my thoughts, Gabby barked at Ben as they tussled, and my happiness bloomed inside me, swelling my chest to bursting.

Gazing out over the fields that looked almost purple in the mist, I knew I'd never give up the sanctuary. I recognized that my doubts had been the product of the short depression that had followed my illness. That's all they were, just rogue thoughts that had seeded in my brain at a time I felt vulnerable and in pain.

The charity's future would always be unsure. Everything would carry on depending upon my gargantuan fund-raising efforts, and I couldn't rest for a moment. There was the forthcoming Christmas Bazaar to think about and plan for . . .

Back at the house later that day, the phone rang. "Hello, this is Barby. Can I help you?"

A woman was sobbing at the other end of the phone.

"We have to rehome our cat. It pees everywhere, and we've tried everything. You have to take her today, we can't cope and there's a baby on the way . . ."

I sighed, saying, "Okay, dear. Does it have to be today?"

"I'm sorry, but yes," the woman said.

Babies were all very well, but why did people feel they had to give up their pets at the same time? The cat obviously either had a medical problem or was reacting to some stresses at home. I heard the resolve in the woman's voice and knew I shouldn't push her. Some people couldn't wait, they rang at breaking point, and might dump the animal somewhere if we didn't step in. Despite that, I wondered, not for the first time, at the ability of people to forget that animals are just as sensitive and in need of care as humans.

"Okay, I'll hand you over to Diane, who will help you, dear," I said, handing the phone to Di.

"Barby, are you there?" It was Dan this time. "You need to come and see this pig, he's a beauty. Another Saddleback we need to find space for."

"Alright, I'm coming. Let me just get my vest on."

I looked around at the people going to and fro outside, Dan my trusty farm manager standing by the back door, Diane with the phone tucked under her chin as she wrote down information about the cat, and I felt a sense of utter contentment wash over me.

"Time for walkies again, Gabby. Now, wait there, gorgeous girl, while I fetch the lead," I said, whistling for the dog, which was a pointless gesture as she was always by my side.

Today, as I sit feeding a baby seagull that was brought to the sanctuary by a member of the public who found it abandoned by the roadside, I know it is a privilege to be of service, as I am every day. I tip tiny amounts of milk into the chick's mouth using a teaspoon, while Gabby sits by my chair, a look of intense concentration on her face. She is gentle with the newcomers, generally sniffing them, knowing to leave them alone while they are nurtured back to health. For someone who has no patience with people, I have endless endurance with creatures such as this seagull, its gawping mouth trembling as I spoon in the liquid.

Just then, Dan poked his head around the kitchen door.

"We've got a holy cow coming in today, I just thought I'd let you know."

"A holy cow—what on earth?" I say to him, bursting out laughing.

"I thought you'd like that. It's not a joke. A Hindu organization in London is coming down today with a white cow that they rescued from a city farm that's shutting down. The best thing is we've decided to have a traditional ceremony, and they're bringing us saris and bindis to wear. You'll probably be garlanded in flowers as well!"

I shrugged.

"If they want to parade me with flowers and silks, then I'm not complaining."

I spooned another mouthful of milk into the seagull's mouth. He was standing inside the cardboard box in which he'd been handed to us. It looked like his wing had been injured, so he was going straight to the vet as soon as he'd had some nourishment.

"Seriously though, Barby. You'll need to dress in a sari and wear a bindi—do you think you can do that?" Dan grinned, pushing his specs up onto his nose.

I smiled in response.

"Anything for an animal. I'll do anything, just like I've always done."

AFTERWORD

By buying this book, each reader is supporting the work of the sanctuary and helping more animals to be saved. I am incredibly grateful to every person who picks up this book and reads it. In doing so, you become part of our story, and another beam of hope in a harsh world. I'd thank you all personally if I could, but I can't. I also need to thank everyone who supports us through donating money, raising funds through races and feats of stamina. It's all those nameless individuals who give us a little each month, who sponsor an animal each year, who do cake sales, plant fairs, and all the jumbles and the donations of animal food or supplies. There are other ways to help us:

Our website, barbykeel.btck.co.uk, shows the dogs and cats that can be sponsored or rehomed, plus there is also the opportunity to donate to the sanctuary.

Please support us. These animals often have no one else to turn to.

Connect with Us

Visit us online at
KensingtonBooks.com
to read more from your favorite authors, see books
by series, view reading group guides, and more.

Join us on social media

for sneak peeks, chances to win books and prize packs,
and to share your thoughts with other readers.

facebook.com/kensingtonpublishing
twitter.com/kensingtonbooks

Tell us what you think!

To share your thoughts, submit a review,
or sign up for our eNewsletters, please visit:
KensingtonBooks.com/TellUs.